SOUL
EVOLUTION

KAMIA SHEPHERD

FriesenPress

Suite 300 - 990 Fort St
Victoria, BC, Canada, V8V 3K2
www.friesenpress.com

Visit **compassionangelcardreading.com** for free audio chapter downloads.

This is a work of Divine Love, any concepts or prayers are recorded
with the utmost respect for all those who share in communion
with the Divine God/dess of the cosmos, and seek to connect and
contribute to the collective consciousness of the universe.

ISBN
978-1-4602-6946-6 (Hardcover)
978-1-4602-6947-3 (Paperback)
978-1-4602-6948-0 (eBook)

1. Body, Mind & Spirit, Spiritualism

Distributed to the trade by The Ingram Book Company

Table of Contents

DEDICATION

This book is dedicated to my fellow brothers and sisters of the planet– the ones who didn't make it, the ones who have struggled, the ones who are struggling now – who continue to be warriors of Light, Divine Love and seekers of Peace. I am with you on this journey. Do not give up, we are almost there.

INTRODUCTION AND THANKS

This book was birthed in the Tetons of Wyoming and nurtured over the course of two years in both Canada and the USA by the loving support of my family of the heart. I thank each of them and hope to encourage their dreams and gifts to the world with the same kindness they have shown to me. To my husband and daughter, it is with honor and Divine Love that I thank the universe every day for gifting this present life with both of you. To my parents who read every line, several times, it would have taken me so many more years to become the woman I am without your love and support. A special thanks to my mother and artist, Jane Shepherd, for generously sharing her soul-deep artwork in the pages of this book. You bring the etheric light into the physical world. To my heart sisters who knew I was writing and encouraged me to keep going: thank you Titania, Rita, Becca, Brea, Danimal, Margo and Melissa. Life is richer for having each of you in it and you inspire me with your strength and passion to make this world a more peace filled place. To my Editor, Jody Lesiuk Carrow, you are the angel I prayed for when I was questioning the value of each word. I cannot wait to read your future book and am ever grateful for the love and polish you placed on this one.

WHAT ABOUT THE SIXTH SENSE?

When a person asks a small child how big they are, many children will stretch their arms out as far as they can, and, straining with the effort of their little chubby arms trying to encapsulate their vastness, declare "SO big." The child is telling the truth. For as they patiently navigate first steps, tumbles and the giant challenge of adult-sized stairs, their spirit is already infinitely larger than their human body. Their bright innocent light is still aware at this stage of childhood that 'they' stretch outwards, upwards and in each direction for miles from their physical body. Their perception of space, the being of human and also this infinite being, is existing in a cooperative manner that allows for intuition and awareness of people they interact with, the environment and elements, and the array of their helpers on the etheric plane: Fairies, Angels, Ascended Masters, God/dess, Earth Spirits and Guides.

In the beginning, when a bright- and light-resonating soul comes into the world in the tiny infant body they will inhabit for this lifespan, there is the first realization of a new perception of space. Sometimes this can bring out a lot of tears. In my case, my parents claim I came out into the world, looked around at them and my siblings, had some breast milk and promptly went to sleep without crying. I believe I was eager and happy in all ways to return to this human existence. On days where I feel several lifetimes old, I think back to this moment and ruefully laugh, for even with several lifetimes of birthing and living and dying, one of the lessons I return to with the occasional outburst of frustration and fist shaking at the sky, is for inhabiting, in the physical body, a small space.

When does this perception of space become confining or 'smaller'? I think each person may have a different time. A trauma, or a hurt, where they felt small all of a sudden, and the giant reach of their spirit felt knocked off center. For myself, as I sat in my grade one desk, clutching rainbow colored pencils, my first negative interaction with space occurred when the teacher wrote on the board, **There are 5 senses**. In my head I said, "What about the sixth sense?" As an intuitive and empathic child looking around at my classmates, many bright eyed and big spirited, I waited to see who would be brave enough to ask the question. There was silence. I chewed on my pencil and waited until lunch to go home and ask my mom why the teacher wasn't talking about the sixth sense, by far my favorite sense, the one I relied upon more than any other to navigate life. I do not remember her response, but it was something along the lines of, "Well, maybe the teacher wasn't told there is one?"

Sharing blogposts, the musings of my sixth sense, I have witnessed an incredible transformation in the way I have interacted with many people in my life, and many beautiful new people I am encountering (for the first time in this life, but 'again' from others.) I spend my favorite time and energy 'speaking' with this writing of 'more', and in celebrating how 'big' we all are. It is my apology and reconciliation to the six year olds from my younger days who got told they were small and equipped with only five ways of knowing the world. It is my apology and reconciliation to the world at large and the adults who are all around me who have been told over and over that they are small.

I recently had a wonderful and spontaneous conversation with a woman about the spirit realm. I thanked her for her 'openness.'

She replied, "Yes, it is true, isn't it? People will speak to the level they are spoken to?" And I agreed, smiling.

The sixth sense can be described in many ways. It can be called 'intuition', 'gut feeling', or 'inner knowing.' It can be described in an extra sensory term such as clairaudience, the ability to 'hear' etheric beings, music or sound. It can be claircognition, the ability to have spontaneous thoughts, ideas and answers to questions that appear in the mind. It can be clairsentience, the communication with light beings, such as Fairies, Angels, Ascended Masters, Spirit Helpers and the elemental kingdom. My sixth sense manifested mostly as clairvoyance, the ability to 'see' images or information from the Akashic Records.

As a child I was vividly aware of other people's emotional and spiritual bodies. Sometimes these appeared as colors surrounding the person. In cases where past life experiences influenced their present life lessons, I saw some of their previous selves super-imposed over their present physical self. I relied on these impressions when meeting new people to assess my level of safety in their presence, and the level of safety for others. Some people – adults and other children - I 'recognized' from previous lives.

This recognition was sometimes painful, other times joyful. Of all my senses, the messages and feelings I received on this level are what allowed me to feel safe. There were moments when a message would come in a fun way, such as in social studies or history class. I enjoyed all class exercises that focused on countries I could 'remember' living in, but occasionally felt frustrated when the information available contradicted something I 'remembered.' I often wanted to speak up about people's emotional bodies, to offer hugs, or discuss the reasons they weren't feeling good, but I also was encouraged by my guides to offer assistance only when asked. My guides helped me navigate this lesson by teaching me how to erect 'shields' so that I could feel less overwhelmed when in school and surrounded by several people. I am grateful for all of the practice in 'shielding' school afforded. Now as an adult, I look back at childhood and marvel at the many helpers, teachers and learning opportunities I encountered. One of the most helpful elements of my childhood for exploring my sixth sense was through living in a National Park. With so much wild space I could let down my shields, saturate in nature and feel, during moments of solitude, my etheric self unfold and expand to its full size.

If I ask my five year old daughter, 'How big are you?' she gets a twinkle in her eye and shouts back, "HUGE!" and then she flexes her chubby arms at me. I hope to have her answer the same way for all the years of her life. I know there will be times when she may not. I see friends and light workers, who have days where their shoulders curl and their heads droop and they speak in small voices, and do not feel the enormity of their spirits and support of their team of angelic realm helpers. I have days where I feel small, too. However, those days have gotten fewer and farther between, and I want to share this feeling, this expansive knowledge that we are 'more' and 'big' and 'beautiful' in our enormous, energy-rich selves.

Here is my prayer for myself, for my child, for each child coming into the world, and for the adults who were once children and told or shown that they did not have light wings:

"I ask that the Angels come into the space that anyone reading these words is inhabiting. I pray that the resonant energy of the Christ Consciousness and the Archangels as messengers and light rays of the Creator/God/dess source of creation be with us each in this moment, and in the way that we are each most receptive to messages, whether through thought, feeling, sound or image. Help us to receive a greater awareness of our Higher Self Selves and auras. Please bring these messages all

day long. Please remind us that we can reach out with these energy selves, to feel rain falling a mile away, to sense people as they come towards us or move away from us. Please help this 'greater awareness' to be gentle and to show us also the incredible tools we have for deflecting and shrugging away all lower energies. Help us to clean the space that we inhabit mentally, emotionally, physically and spiritually. And please help us all to feel energized by this reminder of Greater Self, empowered to act in our daily lives with this knowing. Thank you Angels, Ascended Masters, Fairies, Spirit Guides and Earth Helpers. Thank you. Amen. OM and Aho."

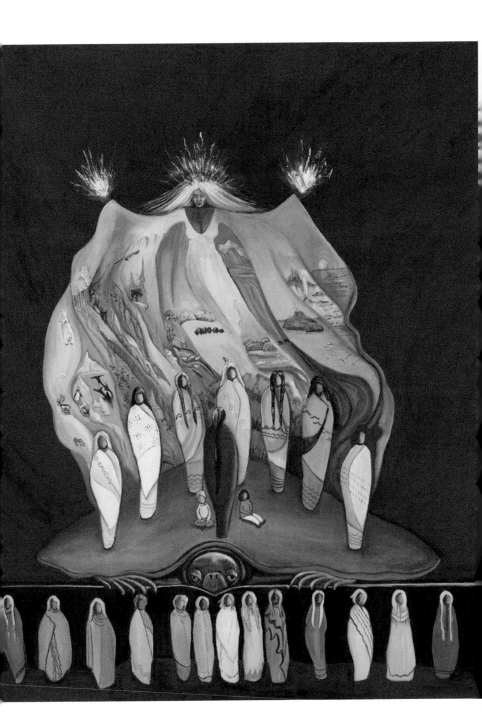

PATHWAYS OF
COMPASSIONATE LIGHT

Coming to the earth plane is a soul level choice that we have all made during our cosmic evolution as incarnated beings at this time. The common threads of light that connect us are brilliant hues of varying vibrations, which have at their center the highest vibration: that of Divine Love. Although many will connect to Divine Love through the modality of different religions with varying names and manners of prayers, I truly believe that when we are connected to God/dess, what we are connecting to is the same radiance, the same light that permeates the universe and shines within us all; what people then choose to do with their inner light, is, of course, governed by the Law of Free Will. We all are given choices daily and throughout our lives to direct our light with free will. This theme repeats in many religions: when in communion with the highest manifestation of Love, we contribute most to the overall positive evolution of our individual lives, our communities, our species and the planet as a whole.

This book is a manifestation of my communion with my Higher Self, the cosmic universe as I perceive it at this time and a desire to communicate an affirmation of our capacity as humans to share in a daily realization of our souls' ability to radiate and attract Love to the benefit of both soul path growth and universal blessings. In simple speak, this book is an exploration of each individual's worthiness and capacity to be loved and express love to others. For 'love' is a word used daily in the 'readings' that I have facilitated for others and the messages I receive from the Angels most often is of teaching and encouraging others to love themselves and therefore share Love with the universe. It is the most prevalent and the 'loudest' message of them all.

Compassion and love for the self affords opportunities to heal our etheric, emotional, mental and physical bodies. Often people carry around an energy mantra of **I am undeserving.** This creates an energy field based on lack and so the energy of the universe that vibrates alongside the person is unbalanced and dim. To connect with pathways of compassionate light is to clear the energy field of the self with positive messages, such as: *I can, I will, I deserve.* This sends out a 'chord' of light to the universe that seeks to connect with the energy matrix uniting all living things: the mountains, the ocean, people, animals and the cosmos at large. Through being kind first to ourselves, feeding our emotional, mental, spiritual, and physical bodies with positive energy and messages, we are able to become an intersection of light that is both supported and aids in sustaining the overall vibration of the universe. The Angels, Ascended Masters and our myriad array of Helpers from the Divine want us to love our Selves so deeply and truly that each cell in our magnificent body begins to vibrate with Love. This is the brightest, loudest, most powerful vibration. We cannot send out these powerful vibrations when we are feeding our own psyche with negative based thoughts. When we invest in ourselves with self-kindness, encouragement, compassion and grace, this personal loving care becomes an investment in the universe at large.

On days where I feel sluggish, unmotivated or sad, I ask my inner child whether she feels loved. Often I receive an intuitive understanding that I need to invest some time and space in a regenerative practice. I practice yoga, read a book, or go for a walk somewhere beautiful. During this investment in self-love, I feel my energy begin to change. My body feels lighter, my mind starts to clear of negative thought patterns, and inspiration, inner joy and enthusiasm begin to blossom once more. When I am feeling joyous, I am able to inspire others. I cannot send out light to the universe for universal healing on days when I need to heal myself. This is a natural rhythm: to refuel and to share afterwards. Our helpers on the etheric realm do not ask us to 'give' every second of every day. They ask us for a balance of giving and receiving. Receiving often means allowing for self-love to saturate our beings once more, so that the compassionate light within us can shine even more brightly.

During this sharing of knowledge and messages from my Angels and Guides, I would like to thank and welcome Archangel Uriel whose soft golden glow has been a patient reminder for me to actually begin writing, Archangel Gabriel who stands patiently behind my keyboard as I work with Archangel Michael to remove my ego's loud fearful thoughts and find a pathway with Archangel Jophiel to the beauty and truth as I am able to realize it and share it with others.

May all who read this be reminded daily that your Angels, Guides, Helpers, Higher Self and connection to God/dess is true and pure and that you are a manifestation of Divine Love in every cell of your body.

In offering of this recognition of the light within us all, I would like to share this affirmation that I have found useful for connecting to my Higher Self and the Light within the Universe:

"Dear Universal Consciousness, Archangels, Guardian Angels, Gods and Goddesses, Ascended Masters and Spirits of the Earth, please help me to recognize the light within others, let me perceive their highest vibrational potential so that I may be reminded of my own highest truth."

Another variation of this affirmation is:

"May I speak, perceive and be a conduit of universal Love in all my actions, and may I forgive myself for the actions as a human that have filled me with guilt or fear, so that in releasing these fears, I make greater space for Love in all that I do. Help me [God/dess, Angels or the Ascended Master you feel most connected to at this time], on all levels to remain grounded into this present reality and incarnation so that I am able to manifest this Love on the physical plane. Amen. Om and Thanks."

We are all powerful healers, light workers and transformational, evolving souls. With the highest respect, I thank you for taking this journey with me and look forward to being inspired by your individual light on our earth, and the cosmic matrix of light future.

CHAPTER ONE

SELF LOVE AND ENCOURAGING

UNDERSTANDING

One of the key steps in the process of self love is to acknowledge that each of us are not only connected to the divine, but that we are all infinitely larger light beings than what our physical bodies express. By this I refer not only to the immense knowledge that many carry from multiple lifetimes on the planet – the basis of the life experience from reincarnations – but also the light beings we return to between incarnations. I am also speaking about the experiences many have brought through from alternate realities, different solar systems and planets. Although each individual has mapped out a different soul path during their present incarnation and each individual will be 'open' to accessing different levels of consciousness as determined by their free will as well as their familiarity with the earth plane, I firmly believe each of us as humans carries a gift of light that is brilliant and expansive. Acknowledging that light within our Selves and one another allows us each to be closer to the vibration and understanding of Divine Love/God/dess.

My mother used to tell me as a child, "Every person has something good about them: find it and focus on that." Although we will all meet and interact with people who challenge us, frustrate or aggravate us, those who may live a life we do not agree with, I still find the directive useful and use it daily. As I pray for the planet and for humanity as a whole, I find something to like, and even love, in those I am most challenged by. This allows for the greatest transformation within myself and in situations globally as well as personally. In praying for people with Love, I have witnessed the powerful energetic and physical planes shift. Love is far more powerful than any fear-based or anger-fueled thought pattern.

How do we learn to love ourselves? Is it an instantaneous transformation that erases all insecurities and fears? Perhaps for some. Is it a daily determination and effort to battle the loud and abrasive ego? For most of us, it will be the latter. The ego will tell us that we are unworthy of love and joy. That truly we are not brilliant, savvy, capable or clever. The first stage of self love, is to make a kind of peace with the ego. Peace is not to agree with all of the negative messages but rather to acknowledge they exist and to determine that the Self, the true Self, is just as capable of sending positive self-messages as the ego. The ego will say everything in the negative. Self-love is encouraged by listening to each of these negatives and creating a positive in response, for example:

EGO: "I couldn't possibly succeed. I am not smart enough, or likable enough, or deserving enough to be given opportunities."

Higher Self: "I have incarnated will and every tool, attribute and brilliance I need in this life to succeed in living to my highest potential. I am Love. I am open to perceiving the numerous opportunities for learning, career, joy and assertive actualization that surround me."

EGO: "I am not special. I am just like, or even less talented and unworthy than everyone else. I should be unhappy because I haven't ever been told, shown or convinced I am worthy of love."

Higher Self: "My unique light shines across time and space. I am an infinite being and connected to all that is Light and Love in the universe. Because I exist, I am worthy of Love. I perceive this Love reflected in nature, other humans and myself every day."

EGO: "I will never release this grief, fear or guilt enough to move forwards. I will be heavy emotionally and this heaviness will remain with my physical body forever. This heaviness of fear and grief is the reason I will not find joy, partnership or fulfillment on my life path."

Higher Self: "I am a light being who carries nothing forward that is not resonant light. Although I honor the emotions I have experienced in this body and other incarnations, I choose to release the fear, the guilt and the lower energies that are blocking me at this time. I ask for assistance from God/dess and Archangel Michael to cut any chords from this and other lifetimes that have held this fear against me. I am ready to release and heal on all levels with the assistance of Archangel Raphael who is a great facilitator of healing and the Ascended Master Quan Yin whose all encompassing spirit of Compassion reminds me I am eternally deserving of healing."

Each individual will have particular ego based fears and challenges to make peace with. I have new fears and challenges daily. I find that if I listen to them calmly and reformulate an affirmation in the positive context, I am no longer controlled or held back by my ego. Some of my reoccurring ego based fears surround sharing my perception of the Divine. I get a nasty inner voice who claims that "No one cares, it's not important." I breathe through these

3

fears, using the sound of a long inhalation and exhalation to center myself and then I reply to my 'ego', "It's important to me, and if it can help empower someone else, it's important to them. I do this with Love." I find that when I am outside in nature, saying the positive affirmation out loud can instantly change my energy and perception. When I am in a crowded room or space with others and if I begin to feel anxious or overwhelmed or shy about communicating my perceptions of the Divine, I set a mental intention that creates a framework for positive energy only. I think to myself, "I will see beauty in this world, I will see beauty and light in these people and myself." Every thought we have has an effect on our perception of the world at large. In times when we feel challenged, unsafe or anxious, we can harness our inner light and make internal choices to alter our experience. We do not need to allow others' experiences and energy to become our experience. We are given the gift of free will to leave situations, thought patterns and experiences that do not resonate with our Highest Good. Like anything that we learn, the more we practice, the stronger we become. I practice positive affirmations every day. It takes very little time to think something positive to ourselves and the more often we do it, the stronger our awareness of our own positive vibrations become. Even four nice thoughts about ourselves a day can alter our realities significantly.

Healthy ways to explore and encourage creating personal affirmations and healing mantras are to write and post the positive version in a place such as the bathroom mirror where it can be seen and read aloud daily. At first there might be the desire, brought on by the ego, to scoff or laugh at the positive affirmation, but the Higher Self has infinite patience and through the repetition of positive thoughts, the Higher Self will always prevail over the ego. Truly, our inner brilliance has patience that spans eons while the ego is confined to the here and now. Our inner brilliance is more powerful. Always. Persevere in committing to the belief that we are lovable, worthy, brilliant and a manifestation of Love/God.

CONNECTING AND ASKING FOR ASSISTANCE:

There are many talented energy healers, holistic therapists, or psychic intuitives who can be extremely helpful in facilitating healing on all levels. Even the greatest spiritual teachers will utilize colleagues and friends to aid them in their own journeys. There is absolute power within each of us to self heal and connect with the Divine on an individual basis, yet asking for help from the God/dess and Angels, with the added facilitation of another person, can be highly effective in creating space for growth.

The messages each person is sent from their Guardian Angels will always be based in Love and encouragement. Likewise, an energy healer, light worker or other professional specializing in facilitating psychic readings and/or healing should always communicate from a place of Love and encourage empowerment of the individual to heal and connect with his/her own inner guidance. It is important to ask God/dess and the Higher Self to give clear indications and be receptive to listening to the Self for emotional and physical responses when seeking a healer.

Some of the tools I have used in the past are finding a light worker who elicits a warm and energizing feeling in my body. If I feel at all ill at ease, I thank them for their time, wish them well on their path and seek an alternative. Just as there are songs that appeal to each of us, so too there are healers and light workers that we will connect with on a different level. Empowering ourselves to trust our instincts and find a healer who resonates with us is vital. There is always the 'right time' and circumstance to bring about the most beautiful and mutual connection for both the healer and the client, and these connections are worth investing energy into and realizing. Trusting our instincts, the right light worker for each of us will validate and encourage our own inner knowing as well as encourage us to expand our consciousness in a healing manner.

As mentioned in the introduction, this earth plane operates under the directives of Free Will. Ultimately we are all responsible for determining the course of our lives, and this includes creating space to receive assistance on any level. During some of the most challenging times in my life I prayed constantly for assistance, and though the results on the physical plane were not as instantaneous as I wished, I did feel instantaneous lightening on the energetic and etheric planes. What follows are some of my favorite affirmations that I have personally found useful. I wish everyone success in connecting with the Light Beings who will be the most clearly communicative to them at this time.

"Dear White Buffalo Calf Woman, please help me to feel my connection to the Earth and the ways in which the Earth has always, and continues, to support me. With respect and Love, I thank the Earth for feeding, housing and providing for me. Please send me clear messages and images that allow me to connect more deeply with my life path and the ways in which I can be of assistance to the planet and Her people at this time. Thank you. Aho."

"Dear Buddha, thank you for your joyous spirit. Thank you for reminding me to perceive and receive the generosity and abundance of gifts that surround me every day on this incredible journey through life. Please assist me in connecting to my own inner joy and to feel confident in sharing this joy with others. Help me to perceive my belly filled with joy by the Universe itself and that the sustenance I need comes not only from food and

words but also from the sunlight and life force of all living things. Please help me to share my light with others, just as you have and always do, with reverence and respect for life. Thank you. Om."

"Dear Christ Consciousness, Archangel Michael and Shiva, please help me to release fear, and receive clear guidance that promotes the safety of myself and loved ones. I ask that God/dess sends Angels and Light to surround me as I navigate this [describe challenging situation] experience and I am open to receiving your assistance and love on all levels. Please help me to connect with my strength and courage and to be grounded into my inner knowing and Higher Self for the safest and the most light-filled transformation. Thank you. OM. Amen."

As a person who remembers past lives and continues to remember others, I have felt a strong connection through previous lifetimes to several Deities, Ascended Masters and Angels. Although in general I continue to believe that the universal energy which has many versions of the title 'God' is one and the same, I also acknowledge the particular resonance that is most helpful in attuning my soul to its path can vary. Sometimes we need the shade from the branches of trees or the pure water of a stream running through sunlight, all within the same forest, to aid in our healing, growth and energy levels. By exploring the terminology that resonates most beautifully with our own soul, we can begin to recognize and honor the ways in which our spirit and self receives sustenance.

Feeling drawn to a different culture's religious or spiritual beliefs is something to be celebrated. Inside the skin we wear in this present life, our radiant spirit remembers wearing other lifetimes' worth of skin color, gender and body shape. For the souls who are new to the earth plane and who do not have other lifetimes of experience to draw on, they possess innate knowledge of living in different energy bodies. All of this knowledge circling the conscious mind can contribute to feelings of being alone and not belonging. I have found it vastly reassuring to meet other people who remember their previous lives or those who can clearly recall the other solar systems they travelled from before becoming human on earth. During a deep meditation or out in nature, I believe we are all offered this same reassurance. When connecting to a Higher Power, by whichever name resonates with us, there truly is a connection of light between us all, and through our journeys we are connected to all other beings resonating light and are never fully separate from this light.

One of my favorite mantras, learned during a yoga teacher training course I took in Northern India is, "SO HUM." Repeated perpetually while in walking meditation or seated in nature, the message, as I understand it, is "I am that, that is I" and "That refers to the universe, the divine in its entirety." It has been a beautiful mantra and tool passed down through generations of yogis and shared with us all. In softly chanting our connection to Divine Love, we encourage our ego to fall silent and create space for all of the resonant Love of the universe to find its way within. May today be a day we remember our own unique resonance and feel it reflected through the universe with love.

CHAPTER TWO

RECOGNITION OF SOULS
WHOSE PATHS WE HAVE CROSSED BEFORE

Connecting with our Soul Paths can be a life long pursuit. For some of us it can be through a daily meditation, like the symbol of the thousand-petal lotus, each prayerful thought peeling away another layer of consciousness to approach the core of light that is our true Divine Soul. For others, Soul Path can be an awareness present since birth, a beacon of purpose which has always fueled our human experience in the present incarnation. For others still, Soul Path can be an intimidating or confusing term, and yet when seeing or hearing it, there is a flicker of curiosity, a *what if* whispering through the mind or heart or body that encourages deeper exploration. In this particular circumstance, when I refer to Soul Path, what I am intending to explore and express is the universal awareness of the highest consciousness of Soul/Light Be- ing and its journey through the cosmos; in particular, its learning opportunities and choices while experiencing the Earth Plane as human.

What is the path of the soul over centuries, or millennia? Where has it been and where is it going? For **all** of us, the answers will vary, but I will frame this chapter within my own experiences. I will also offer the exploration of others who may have had a similar awareness of reincarnation as it spans through many conscious realities, star grids and lifetimes, like so many shooting stars.

When we have a dream, image, strong feeling of recognition that a person we are interacting with is familiar from a previous lifetime, then chances are very good we have indeed had a previous lifetime with them. Faith in our own instincts is essential, though seeking validation through visiting an energy worker, ANGEL THERAPY PRACTITIONER (R), or other psychic intuitive, are helpful tools to reaffirm our instincts. Most people will continue to cycle through several lifetimes with the same souls in their life orbit. Some of these interactions will be uncomfortable and some will be filled with loving opportunity. Many will continue to repeat themselves until the karmic debris resulting from the interactions is healed or transformed.

Consciousness can have a sense of humor. For truly one of the best ways of changing the energy in the room is when people allow themselves to have a beautiful and spontaneous laugh. One of the more influential clairvoyant women I met as a child had a laugh that sounded like a ringing bell. She would be speaking to a group of people and throw her head back in mid-sentence and let her laughter reverberate across the room. And even though the subject matter was serious, people would start to smile as the energy would instantly change. Several years later, when I travelled to Rishikesh, India, the yogi whom I studied with often asked us to engage in spontaneous laughter at the end of a yoga class. I always felt sheepish and awkward, forcing out those first initial laughs, squeezing my eyes tightly so as not to feel embarrassed that others might see how truly forced my laughter sounded. Swift on the heels of that thought, however, would come actual laughter and soon the entire class would be belly laughing. As a group, our auras would expand from internal exploration to external interaction and sharing in a dynamic energy between us all.

Sometimes when I have a past life memory, dream or spontaneous realization during an inter- action with another human, I find that reminding myself to see the humor in the cosmic forces and choices that brought me into a circle of interaction with a particular soul for another round *is* the best 'medicine.' One of my favorite male friends I met in this life on a crisp, cold morning in Northern India. Both of us had bundled up in scarves, winter hats and mittens. As our eyes met and we shook hands, I had a spontaneous memory of being dancing girls together in a harem in a past life. The memory was of a very hot, sultry climate and as we both stood stomping our frozen toes and trying to warm up, I started to laugh, feeling blessed to be reunited with a dear friend in a new place.

In gaining valuable knowledge surrounding why the soul interaction is occurring once more, why certain lessons in life with another person are surfacing, the best healing tool I have learned for clearing karmic debris is first to recognize a past Soul relationship, thank my Higher Self for the opportunity to grow and heal through making different choices in this life and remaining in the Light, as well as by maintaining a healthy sense of humor when the situation is particularly challenging. As examples of some of the most pivotal learning opportunities past life Soul interactions have afforded in this life, I offer three different personal experiences. The names of the individuals are absent out of respect for their privacy and personal Soul Paths.

FAMILY AND SOUL GROWTH

One of my close family members I remember from two previous lifetimes. While I enjoy revisiting these particular lifetimes in some aspects, the challenges my family member and I occasionally have are reminiscent of karmic debris created in our shared past. I am grateful for the ability to access the lifetimes we have shared previously and currently as both offer valuable lessons I need to encourage my growth and our relationship during this lifetime.

In the first lifetime together, I was a woman who lived in a village in Europe who shared herbal lore, aided in midwifery and gave readings for children when they were born so that their parents knew what paths they were most likely going to be drawn to during their incarnation. My present family member manifested in that time as a very devout male religious figure thoroughly committed to the witch trials. He came to my village when I was in my early twenties and I was put on trial and then killed. The interaction in this life generated fear surrounding speaking words associated with the Divine. In this present lifetime, as I began to build confidence about sharing my clairvoyance, I experienced fear of speaking about my perceptions whenever this family member was around. Suffice to say, the end of my life during the previous lifetime was not a pleasant one, and when the priest incarnated again it was with a different set of lessons for a gentler exploration of connection to "God".

In the second lifetime we shared, we were both monks in a Tibetan monastery. Our entire lifetimes were dedicated to a meditative existence. I was an older male monk and passed when his soul was just barely an adult. In this lifetime we spoke very rarely but shared a deep reverence for the Divine. The words I spoke in this lifetime were received with a desire and openness to learn by this person, a direct opposition to the initial life where my words were silenced with force. As I was much older, and his soul encountered mine as a child for the first time, I felt joy at sharing the vibrations of the sacred mountains with him and a more balanced incarnation grew. In this life, I was able to die of natural causes and heal an aspect of the previous life together, as the soul witnessed my peaceful death but was not the cause of it in any way. The monastery where he lived was eventually destroyed and many of the monks were slaughtered. In this life he was put to death for his beliefs, just as I had died for mine during the first encounter.

When our souls decided to incarnate together during this present lifetime, my family member and I created another learning opportunity. Although we do not share a dialogue surrounding the Divine, or an identical ideology, what I have appreciated learning from our interaction is that assertiveness and aggression are two separate things. When we first met, several lifetimes ago, I was silenced through force. When next we met in Tibet, I learned the power of silence through divine devotion and shared this as an older monk with the younger ones. In this third lifetime, I was always encouraged to have a clear, communicative and assertive voice by my family member who is an advocate of healthy aggression such as physical exercise and positive assertiveness through verbal articulation. When we disagree, I remember our first lifetime, the black coat he wore, and I breathe through the fearful aspects of sharing my knowledge and focus on allowing that our present journeys differ. When we are in synthesis, we share laughter and delight and I see an image of his monk self, superimposed over his present visage, smiling. Our relationship continues to evolve and we both endeavor to have tolerance for one another whenever a spiritually based conversation might arise. My family member shares gifts of grounding with me through a continued life in the mountains and I share aspects of the free spirited gypsy I once was, encouraging him to explore the world. Through Love we continue to heal our past karma along our individual soul paths.

FRIENDSHIP AND KARMIC LESSONS

I became friends with another child when I was six and remained steadfast friends for several years. In this lifetime, we are the same age and had many similar interests. I often felt, however, that I was responsible for the emotional wellbeing of this friend, particularly in terms of sustenance of happiness, loyalty and, on the physical plane, of feeding. Even as children, I was constantly opening our fridge and offering my friend something to eat. As a Taurus, a lover of food and flavor, in this life I now delight in feeding friends and sharing wonderful food with anyone. With this particular relationship however, even at the age of six, I felt a strong compulsion to feed my friend.

The friend often made emotional demands of loyalty and unconditional love that left me feeling taken advantage of and wounded. During this challenging time together, I prayed for a dream which would clarify the previous life we had shared together and the healing needed for us both to continue on happily in this present one. I prayed my Higher Self would help me find clarification about this relationship. During a lucid dream, I `saw' that during a lifetime in Eastern Asia, I had been this friend's father and we had been very poor fisherman. Riding in a boat when this friend - who was then my son - was about seven, I lost our nets and leapt into the water to try and recover them. Exhausted from a lack of food and pulled by stormy water and the strong current, I was able to hoist a fish into the boat, but slipped from my son's grasp and drowned. In this life, I was still carrying the guilt of having abandoned my son, and had a compulsive desire to nurture, feed and support this friend.

I spent several years praying that our karmic debt could be healed. Occasionally I still have to resist the urge to ask this friend whether he/she is getting enough to eat, even if we haven't conversed for several months. What praying for this peace between us has done is enable me to stop feeling so responsible for my friend's well being. Our friendship is no longer close and I take this as an indication that the prayers were effective. We have other paths to explore during our current lifetimes, and though the beginning of this one was made richer by that person's presence, I am at peace with our individual growth apart in recent decades.

ROMANTIC RESONANCE AND MOVING FORWARD

In my mid-twenties, I encountered one of my most pivotal relationships. I had been (and still am) searching for a greater understanding of my place on the planet. Although I had a few close individuals whom I shared a spiritual dialogue with, for the most part life, and human interaction, felt like a constant balance of trying to not say things that would make people think I was crazy. I felt lonely often and longed to connect more deeply with a romantic partner in a manner that allowed for an honest dialogue about previous lives and our present journeys. My previous relationships were characterized by an attraction to who the person/ soul had previously been so that I could heal karmic lessons from the past, instead of being able to meet and celebrate one another fully in the present.

I met a young man of whom I carried an incredibly strong memory of living and loving with during one of my earliest lifetimes in ancient Samaria. I received the flash of recognition over a group dinner, a vivid memory of us together in a palace. Sure that I was encountering yet another person who would not remember 'me', I excused myself and went home early in hope of sorting through the emotions the memory had released. I had deeply loved this soul. My sense of self preservation, and ego, asserted a pretense that we only 'knew' each other from the past few days and that he was going to be detrimental to my emotional health through a lack of recognition. So I decided, and I can see the humor in this now, to avoid any interactions with him in the future.

The following day he tracked me down and offered me a coffee. To my eternal delight, he then related a dream he had just awoken from and his similar reaction of wanting to avoid ever seeing me again. Instead, he decided he would choose the courageous path and admit to a similar memory of a previous life. We laughed about the differences in the lives we had 'chosen' in this present incarnation, the frustrations and gifts that they and the previous ones had afforded, and both got to feel and acknowledge the powerful healing of that joint confirmation. The initial life we remembered was one of my first incarnations on the planet in physical form. During this life we had been separated when those that wished to usurp his power poisoned me and buried me in the desert. All to cause him pain. He had carried the loss with him through several lifetimes and still felt guilt over the death. During our conversations, as we communicated about the ways the memories impacted our present interactions, we were able to celebrate the undying aspects of the soul, and one another, as well as heal the karmic debris we each had been carrying.

This was the first time I had ever had an absolute reassurance that a past life memory I was having was not simply a figment of my vivid imagination, as my ego has always been quick to assert. The level of confidence this interaction built in my own trust in spiritual experiences has led to many new and beautiful levels of joy in this life. I will always be appreciative of the powerful influence and soul-healing relationship this encounter afforded.

Though I have remembered many lives and expect that I will encounter more as I continue to interact with the fascinating Souls wandering across this dynamic planet and time, the three illustrated above have a similar theme that I have found valuable. Through acknowledging and having faith in my perceptions of my own Soul's evolution, I was better able to understand my present life and the gifts I could share with others. Through forgiveness of both my own previous life choices as well as those made by others' Souls, I was better able to receive and share healthy Love in this present life. With forgiveness and Love I was ultimately able to release the relationships that had served their purpose and honor and allow for karmic healing.

On any pathway towards illumination, spiritual understanding and Divine Love, I believe some tools remain universal. Through faith in our own perceptions and in our ability to grow and to evolve, we empower others to have faith within themselves for their own spiritual journey. Through forgiveness, first of ourselves, we are better able to forgive others and encourage their individual journeys. I do not use the term forgiveness to mean the condoning of harmful behavior, but rather of forgiveness in the sense that we can accept something has occurred and move forward from it, having learned something valuable. We can move with a determination to bring more Light into the world by living our own Soul Path with a focus of sharing and receiving Light and Love.

An affirmation and prayer I have found useful during many past-life relationship interactions:

> **"Dear Creator/God/dess, please help me to see clearly the ways in which a past life with this person is influencing our present interaction. Please send me clear dreams or messages to help me understand how we can mutually heal from the karma we have jointly created. Please send Archangel Michael to cut any chords of fear that attach us from this or any previous lifetimes so that only the light of Divine Love remains between us. I ask that healing on all levels occur at this time, and should our lives now take separate pathways, I ask that we do so with Angelic assistance and forgiveness on a Soul level. Please send the loving compassionate energy of Quan Yin, Archangel Raphael and Jesus to help us to individually and universally heal. Thank you. Amen. Om. Aho."**

Any variation of this prayer with the ascended master or deity we are most drawn to working with at this time will bring light. The affirmation is powerful by centering on healing, forgiveness and release of any fear, suffering or pain. With healing often comes acceptance that a part of the healing may be moving forward beyond the present relationship to either a healed healthy one, or to separate lives entirely. With Light, and respect for our journeys, may these lessons bring gentleness, renewed purpose and more a expansive understanding of Love into our lives.

CHAPTER THREE

REBIRTH, DEATH AND DYING: WARMING THE SPIRIT AND RECHARGING THE LIGHT

Much of what Western media culture depicts is that death and the spirit world are to be feared. We can see movies or read books made about vengeful ghosts or people desperate to find the answer to 'eternal youth' and avoid death all together. Yet in many indigenous cultures, death is perceived rather like a doorway into another realm of existence and that 'the other side' is filled with Light. My understanding is that the Aboriginal Peoples in North America, are given guidance from ancestors and relatives who have passed over. The guidance is filled with loving and empowering messages.

Although each person must seek the answer to their own beliefs throughout their lifetimes, in this chapter I will explore the concept and belief that death is a bridge, ushering a Soul across as it transcends the physical plane and rejoins the myriad network of Light connecting the cosmos.

The beauty of this light expansion is that a Soul will reunite itself with a greater knowing of its own divine brilliance, it will also retain the connections of Love it made on the planet and a resonance of its experience during its past lifetimes. The Akashic Records, those etheric records of all that has been, are a compilation of each individual soul's evolution as well as all the knowledge gathered throughout their lifetimes and experiences.

Many people fear when their loved ones depart from this world that they are never to be in existence again. Yet even science will agree that matter neither disappears nor appears. It simply changes form. In this way, it is my belief that the Light that makes up the essence of a human continues beyond death, indeed it expands and multiplies and resonates through the Universe, shining towards those who infused it with Love during their earth-walk.

Perhaps a person hears a song that reminds them of a departed loved one, or smells a dish that was the person's favorite, or even sitting in the sunlight, suddenly feels as if a loved one is beside them, or the corner of their eye catches an image of the loved one walking near them. All of these impressions are not figments of the imagination. Light Beings are not confined to the physical realm, or time or space, and they attempt to send messages of Love and support all the time. If we are open to receiving Light-filled messages, or granting ourselves the ability to experience healing, these messages can effect incredible change.

For almost two decades I have felt the presence of my grandfather who passed when I was fourteen. I have found the presence of his Light quite powerful and though this Soul made choices as a human I did not agree with in many respects, his energy on 'the other side' - so to speak - has taught me much about the boundless energy that is a Light Being's core essence, the expansive connection it has in both sending Light to those it encountered during its last incarnation, how it supplies valuable insights regarding the evolution of a Soul as a whole and the ways in which fulfilled karmic agreements during life affect a Soul. For example, when my grandfather was a child, he met a native man who shared with him valuable lessons on how to survive and build strength. The native man taught my grandfather to run for several miles with a small pebble beneath his tongue to conserve the moisture in his mouth and body when water was not available. Their two Souls were old friends from a previous life in ancient China. In that lifetime, they had been comrades in arms and helped one another survive. The karmic imprint of my grandfather having protected this Soul in battle allowed for a resonance to continue forward in the life they encountered one another in again. In my grandfather's life, this and other lessons shared by the native man later helped him to survive the two years he spent in a POW camp in World War II.

Soon after this grandparent's passing, I began to perceive a giant golden orb of light whenever I thought of him. This globe of light was often accompanied by images of life experiences during the Soul's incarnation as well as images of light connections occurring in the etheric realm. I saw flashes of his life when he made joyful choices such as having a family with my grandmother; I saw flashes of war experiences that were filled with sorrow. I also saw the ways in which his soul reached towards the earth, connected to the light of humans still alive, ones he lent support to such as his son's and grandchildren. The light arcs appeared like ribbons of gold, reaching down to lend strength to those experiencing danger or adversity. Because of the choices he made during his life walk, I am much more comfortable when it is images of the etheric plane that are communicated. Whereas during his lifetime there was an addiction with alcohol that lead to violence, in the etheric plane I am better able to perceive the strengths of the Soul as an evolving being and so, over the years, I have become more comfortable communicating and receiving guidance from this Soul. When I am in adverse physical conditions, whether traveling or out in nature alone, I can feel the Soul's presence helping me to chose a safe path. When I made the choice to give up consumption of alcohol in my mid twenties, it was with the support of this Soul who 'showed' me the energetic deterioration of his connection to his own internal Light during his lifetime as my grandfather by drinking. The Soul does not ask for me to condone choices made in his most recent life. The Soul shows me what 'was' and encourages me to make choices personally that will strengthen my connection to my own Soul Path and inner Light. In this manner, I am better able to reconcile the recent incarnation and the greater Light Being.

During any communication with the etheric realm, particularly with a deceased loved one, Archangel Michael and his Angels, with the support of the Divine, send protective Light and Love to block any lower energies that might be near. Archangel Michael is a limitless light energy available to anyone and everyone regardless of what religious belief system they are most comfortable with. I have found his energy to be similar in color - brilliant blue - and light to Shiva. Wearing this color, as well as visualizing a globe of light surrounding and protecting a person, can bring an instantaneous relief from fear.

Although many images in the media assure us that 'ghosts' are often tragic or malevolent beings, this is not always the case. Though lower energies exist, we are able to create a framework which allows for only Light Beings to communicate with us. We do this by seeking assistance through prayerful meditation. Many expanded souls such as Ascended Masters Jesus, Quan Yin, Buddha and various Saints do exist on the etheric realm and are happy to provide guidance, loving support and encouragement for any who request it. By asking to have one of the Ascended Masters, in conjunction with Archangel Michael, aid and assist us in receiving only positive vibrational information and messages of Light from departed loved ones, the energy is given a framework that can only allow for safe and beautiful information. If at any time there is fear, a sense of cold or unease, then Archangel Michael will use a 'Sword of Light' to surround us and protect us in all ways. Here is an example of when my fears, and the messages that I was receiving, were assisted through prayer:

In my early twenties I liked to hike alone with my dog. We would wander along trails and explore places together with a backpack of snacks and a journal. During one of my wanders, I was in a meditative state, having spent the entire morning walk admiring beautiful landscapes of rolling plains and mountains in the distance. We came to a place I had not seen before and I decided it would be a good spot to sketch and write. I made a comfortable seat for myself against a boulder. While drawing, I received an impression that the land I was sitting on was the site of a battle that had happened over seventy years ago. I could sense and 'see' the people who had been. I could see where they had fallen. At first this image felt very overwhelming and frightening. My breath quickened. I could feel my body tense. I started to pray for Light to surround and protect me and with each prayer for change in energy, I became more aware of the way the sunlight warmed and comforted my skin and how the wind gently stirred the smells of the grass and plants around me as well as the sweet creek water which was nearby.

My prayers worked to 'ground' me into that moment in that place. When I became more centered, the image of the battlefield persevered but was now overlaid with the present landscape. I was no longer held transfixed by all the death, by the details of the men who had fallen. A young native man's spirit came to sit near me. He did not fill me with fear and he gestured to the landscape around us. At the time, I was very shy about receiving or communicating any messages in the role of a 'medium' and so I continued to pray that only light would be with me. In this way, he continued to communicate but from a distance where I was no longer overwhelmed.

As I prayed for those who had fallen, I asked that their Spirits be guided and aided into becoming the Light and remembering the Light that had once been. The gift the young man offered me was a very profound vision of transformation on a Soul level of the men from the battlefield. He showed me where the men and horses had fallen and died – their imprint, so to speak – a recorded memory in this world now of their falling. He showed me their bodies had become the Earth. Because their deaths had been violent, this imprint remained; but in the same manner, those who had died at peace with their lives also left a trace of their passing. Sitting in the sunlight, I could perceive arcs of light moving from where the memory of the bodies lay out into the mountains, the trees and to the stars beyond. Some of the Spirits had chosen to stay closer to the earth realm, in communion with and offering guidance to their children and generations of children who follow. Some of the Lights returned to their star systems to share the knowledge they had gained during their lives in bodies on the earth. Still others had returned to bodies in new incarnations with a memory, an Akashic record, which brought forward their experience on the earth plane in different cultures, colors of skin and gender. Whichever pathway their Light had chosen, the imprint of their lives here, the memories of the essence of the people they had been, remained recorded in Earth's perfect memory and the Akashic Records.

What on the surface had been an image that I found frightening, I 'saw' transformed into something very beautiful and I thanked the young Spirit Guide who had offered me the gift of an alternate perspective. For as the world evolves, and we with Her, the Divine Consciousness of the planet exists as both a physical being that cradles and houses us, but also as an etheric being that is connected through networks and pathways of Light across the vast Cosmos and Universe; and the pathways, the geometric arcs of light, are not confined by our present world's constructs of time.

Just as people can dream of a past life, so too can Earth remember the beings who have always walked through a forest or across a mountaintop. And should that mountaintop have once been a cavern in the depths of an ocean that has long since dried, then so too does Earth remember the sea creatures that swam across those caverns and spaces now occupied by air. Time is both linear as we experience it now in the human realm, but also circular: just as the world is round, so too do the Souls who ignite our living experience have the ability to see around the arc of their evolution and the evolution of others.

It is a time on the planet when many people are beginning to discover their curiosity as well as a deep wealth of knowledge to draw upon from previous life experiences and star systems. It is an incredible 'time' for people to begin to have faith in their own inner knowing of both their own Soul's evolution and to support and celebrate the evolution of the planet and one another.

In places where trauma has occurred, there are memories of this trauma. Sending Love to a place and time, regardless of when in 'history' it occurs, does in fact add a healing layer of energy to the circumstance. People receive prayers on a Soul level. As a highly visual person, I interpret a prayer like a beam of rainbow radiance, encapsulated in white light, reaching out through time and space to another Soul/person. Just as we can heal trauma that we have experienced in a present life through prayer, love and determination – in the sense that we no longer feel as 'wounded' by an experience – so too can Earth (and the Souls who have walked across Her) feel the healing from our intentions of Divine Love and Light.

Fascinating experiments have been done regarding the effects of energy, prayer and music on water, such as Masaru Emoto's *The Hidden Messages in Water*.[1] Molecules change when we send prayers to them. When a person is praying toward their own healing process, the water molecules, the cells of their body begin to vibrate in unison with the prayer. I have 'seen' illness in my own body transform through intentional prayer, as well as in clients, who, by sending their awareness to an injury on their bodies, transform what is occurring on physical, mental, emotional and spiritual levels. The cells seek to resonate at their highest potential. As we purify our thoughts, the cells can mirror our intentions of love, healing and wellness. Beaming Love towards the water in the cells of our bodies can create balanced, healthy and beautiful cells. Just as beaming negative thoughts and vibrations can alter the perfection of our cells.

The environment and the planet feels prayer and intentions for greater light and healing and so do we. A Soul out in the Light network can also perceive a prayer, such as a brilliant light sent to them, or a healing vibration of music that joins with their own unique resonance. Praying to heal a trauma that has occurred to Earth or the people on Her does help in the evolution and healing of that which is being prayed for. Each time intentional light is sent out into the Universe, so too is the light of the sender amplified and expanded.

To explore a way of transforming energy, here is a simple process to try:

➤ In the morning, light a candle and spend a few moments deepening your breath. Ask that your Higher Self be more grounded into your physical being in this moment. Take long inhales, envisioning each lung filling with healing hues of light, like morning sunlight, and that the light is clearing and healing all of the cells in our bodies.

When you have taken at least eight deep breaths, drink a glass of water and ask the water to flush any toxins our body no longer needs out of it. Next, grab your broom and sweep out the room you have been sitting in. Ask that the Angels, particularly Archangel Jophiel, the Ascended Masters White Tara or Lao Tzu to assist you in clearing out the energy of the room.

When the room has been swept, return to the candle and spend a few more moments in contemplative mediation. This is an excellent opportunity to focus on what energy and intentions you would like to set for the day. If you are comfortable writing, give yourself the gift of a few minutes of journaling anything that 'pops' into mind. Or if you are artistically inclined, use these moments to play music or to paint, draw or dance.

The purpose of this simple exercise is to explore how a room in our own home is effected and affected by creating a few moments for 'sacred space', for integration of our Higher Self into our present being and for clearing the energy of previous day to create space for the new energy we would like to experience during this day. If this exercise brings more vitality and positive space for healing during our day, then consider – what would a few moments of focused intention and prayer do on a larger scale? What if humanity collaborated to pray and cleanse sites on the planet that have been polluted or experienced human trauma? What if fields where people died became sights of prayer, reverence and the many dancing, singing or painting together? How would the planet and the Souls who had 'memories' of that space through time 'feel' or experience Light if healing and Love was sent and overlaid?

On most days, I remember to set an intention, to start the day with prayer regardless of the pace of life that may distract me or take me somewhere beyond my comfort zone, room or house. I always experience a difference in the way I perceive the world and those around me if I have taken this time. Other ways of cleansing space can be through prayer or through smudging the space with incense or sage. People also clear their space with sound, music and crystals. I find that the act of sweeping is not only practical but a nice, moving meditative way to 'clear my space.' Whatever tools we are drawn towards for clearing our own personal space and energy, we need to be conscious as we use them, and in doing so, we will notice the ways in which our personal vitality and energy changes as we utilize them. If our day affords other moments, take some of that sacred clear space we have fostered within our being and send a prayer out into time and space, that others, loved ones, or the planet itself experience healing and clarity.

Our prayer matters. Our Souls are infinite and we have the power in our thoughts, actions and intentions to a/effect positive change through time and space.

References:

1. Emoto, Masaru The Hidden Messages in Water. OR: Beyond Words Publishing, 2004

CHAPTER FOUR

SOUL MATES AND ROMANTIC
RELATIONSHIPS

There are different layers and light connections two Souls can make during their interactions on the earth plane to constitute a 'Soul level' relationship. Often a 'Soul Mate' is referred to as the romantic partner with whom a person combines their energy to achieve a balanced and harmonious level of awakening for each individual. This union, and combination of unique frequencies, also encourages all those the Soul Mate relationship interacts with to benefit from the unique combination of Light they have created and continue to sustain one another with. The Soul Mate relationship in a romantic partnership is an incredibly powerful and beautiful relationship to experience. Romantic Soul Mates are not the only type of soul mates that can effect positive change and elevation of the overall 'frequency' of the planet, however. Souls who connect and combine their energies can occur in a powerful and beautiful way through both friendships and working relationships.

During the time that a person is incarnated on the planet, they may encounter Soul friends from previous lives, people who inspire them to honor the path they have chosen to walk in this life, bringing forward gifts from previous lives and star systems. They may also attract a Soul-deep relationship in a coworker with whom they go on to accomplish great things with, achieving their like-minded intentions for the planet and the evolution of humanity. What all of these Soul level encounters and relationships have in common is that it is the highest vibrational intention of the individual souls to encourage the manifestation of their own, and one another's, dreams, Soul purpose and gifts, into the earth realm. It is why they are drawn together. Through their interactions, their combined energies nourish their individual energy and each individual's unique resonance is made clearer.

HONORING OUR OWN SOUL PATH, RESONATING THROUGH TIME AND SPACE

We each come to the planet with particular gifts and light to share. Some of us may do this on a day-to-day basis by sharing light through each of our daily interactions. Perhaps we are someone who gives out beautiful smiles as a checkout attendant at a toll-booth, supermarket or campground. Perhaps we bring gifts of music and artistic expression, inspiring others to take a chance with their own gifts and to embrace the ways in which they uniquely interpret the earth. Still others of us will bring gifts of kindness through parenting or service to humanity as aid or medicinal workers. Whatever the scale or reach of human interaction, each unique light is just as precious as every other.

Thanks to a musically minded husband, I perceive us all as a grand symphony, as instruments of light with our own unique sound, yet when combined, absolutely magnificent. But to truly work with all of the interconnectedness of the Love and brilliance with one another, it is first key to nurture, recognize, and celebrate our own Divine gifts. In so doing, we unconsciously inspire and support others in their own shining and we ourselves become a light which ignites limitless other lights. For it is when we are shining in our own truth, celebrating others for the ways in which they shine, we begin to send out a beacon of light and sound that allows us to attract the Soul Mate relationships that will continue to encourage our own Soul's path and open up new pathways of light to explore with each other.

Committing to celebrating the Self can be a daunting task. Many people will explore ways of presenting themselves or interacting with the world that are not truly aligned with who they feel they are. This can be a defense mechanism so that when we experience rejection, we can assure ourselves that we are being rejected for qualities that aren't the 'real me.' It takes tremendous courage to present the world with our true Self, courage to allow that people may not understand our true Selves, be supportive or understanding in the ways that we yearn for them to be. The rewarding aspect of presenting our true Self to the world that can offer the most reassurance, however, is that though people may pass from our lives, in being truly and authentically who we know ourselves to be, we will attract new people and opportunities from friendship, family of the heart and healing. The most attractive people I have met are the ones who express themselves with authenticity. They inspire me to do the same and their presence resonates throughout time and space.

What are the things, words, motions, sounds or colors we would express to the world if we felt absolutely supported and loved? These are the important questions to ask, especially when yearning to interact with a Soul Mate relationship. For some people, beginning to do those things, say those words and make those healthful changes are enough of a beacon to send out to the universe that then attracts a Soul Mate relationship. For as we allow our Light to shine, we empower our Soul Mate to do the same. It takes two people who are committed to themselves, and their path, to form a Soul Mate union. And when an individual begins to invest in themselves in this way by speaking their personal truths and sharing their gifts, somewhere, out in the world, their Soul Mate is supported in doing the same.

As a highly sensitive individual, I often despaired of ever finding my Soul Mate. I also spent a lot of my time and energy trying to disguise who I really was, afraid that the hyper sensitivity to other dimensions of reality would absolutely assure me a lifetime of rejection and disapproval. Not only did I often feel lonely in relationships, I denied myself the balm of Self Love by continuing to repress in almost all social situations my authentic Self. In my mid twenties, after extricating myself from a particularly unhealthy relationship, I made a commitment to myself to become more of who I truly sensed myself to be. I started practicing yoga and mediation with crystals daily and investing in myself through healing energy work with trusted facilitators. I spent six months dedicated to 'Me.' I read the books I wanted and ate the food that nourished me. I fostered friendships based on my authentic Self and began to blossom. I explored my own psyche and decided once and for all, I would rather have a very limited base of social interactions, ones that actually nourished me, than a wider scale that did not. I also allowed for communication with my Angels and Guides in a less inhibited manner than in the previous years. What they repeatedly told me was, "You have to believe you deserve something before you can attract it." I also repetitively heard: "You have to be agreeable to growth and expansion with Love."

It wasn't comfortable to look at the ways in which I had allowed my ego to convince me that previous relationships were all I deserved. It was also rather uncomfortable to look at the ways in which I had barricaded myself off from Love. Small changes, like surrounding myself with flowers to remind me that all things must grow to blossom, were ways in which I honored these messages. Going for long hikes to see the world from new perspectives and remember the healing power of nature also honored this.

A few months into my 'me time', I went to a women's writer's conference in New Mexico. I took time off from work, planned the whole thing in less than a week, and sped off to the red rock country surrounding Santa Fe to immerse myself in female energy and honor my impetus to write. While there, I met many inspiring women and one of them offhandedly commented that she thought I was the perfect romantic match for her neighbor. Given that she and her neighbor lived in an entirely different country from me, this seemed interesting, but also like something I could easily dismiss.

The universe was not finished with me nor with my friend's neighbor. A few months later, after a series of emails, phone calls and finally with meeting face to face, I received the most Soul deep gift: that of meeting my Soul Mate on the earth plane. From the first encounter, I felt inspired and supported in being my absolute authentic Self. It was a tremendous relief to be accepted when speaking about the etheric realm. I felt as if in being in the presence of this bright Soul, I was finally able to shine, just as I truly was.

Our relationship progressed, facing challenges along the way, yet with one another these challenges have been manageable and made me more appreciative of my partner's strengths and gifts. I celebrate his individuality and we encourage each other to follow our dreams. We make compromises and we weather the occasional storm. Being near him is a relief, a balm to my spirit and an encouraging song of delight. I endeavor to walk my own Soul Path, to grow,

to feel worthy of love and to write, honoring the `truest me' by upholding my ability to shine and inspire him.

HONORING YOUR LIGHT

I wish this gift of Light and Selfhood on all who read this chapter. I pray that in committing to being who you really feel you are, you attract the connections and Soul-deep relationships – whether friendships, coworkers or romantic partners – that inspire and support your own brilliance.

"Dear Great Spirit, Universal Consciousness and Higher Self, please send me assistance through (any Archangels, Deities, or Ascended Masters you feel most aligned with) and Light so that I may find the courage to offer the gifts I have brought to the planet at this time, out into the world, where they may nourish and inspire others to shine. Please help me to heal my self-esteem, to feel worthy of love and healing and to know that I am a beautiful Soul and a beautiful person worthy of partnership on all levels. Thank you. Amen, Aho and OM."

When we are honest about ourselves, we will find it easier to see others honestly. If we can acknowledge that we have moments of insecurity, of self-doubt as well as moments of daring, celebration and magnificence, we empower others to do the same. Finding the things we like about ourselves, finding ways to accept the ways in which we believe we have let ourselves down, are all useful and important tools in the nourishment of Self-discovery and actualization.

The ego will assert the negative; your Angels and Guides will assert the positive. A true Soul Mate-based relationship will support you in your growth and evolution. This does not mean that each new stage of growth will be comfortable, but rather, there will be an inner knowledge and a supportive voice which encourages you to continue to grow. In this growth comes the opportunity for a greater union of Light. Just as you are a strand of Light, so is your partner, and when your Lights combine they make a dynamic spiral reaching out into the Universe, investing in greater Love for humanity as a whole.

When one of you feels like they are not shining, the other can ask questions such as, "What do you want to change about your life to bring about a greater sense of Self knowledge?" and, "What can we do as a couple to create space for your life purpose?"

Bringing awareness and focus to how each individual contributes to the whole is a healthy and Love-inspiring tool to promote relationship and personal health. Some days, the answers to those questions could be as simple as, "I want to watch a funny movie and remember to laugh more." Some days they might be, "I want to change our lifestyle so that we spend less and have more time for investing in our creative pursuits." When the answers and the questions are promoting change, we must remember to ask for Angelic assistance and to pray for that which we wish to manifest together.

Here is a soul mate-inspired prayer:

"God/dess, please send your assistance and Love to my partner right now. Please send the light of Archangel Jophiel and the ascended master Aphrodite, to aid him/her in finding his/her own inner beauty, and Archangel Michael for overcoming fear and remembering how brilliant he/she truly is. Please send reminders every day of his/her own inner power, so that he/she feels confident in his/her gifts and can navigate these life changes with the most grace possible. Thank you. Amen, Aho, and Om."

When we pray for someone to reconnect with their own inner power, we do not create a negative or codependent pattern, but instead inspire healing and Self Love. When we love ourselves, we have greater amounts of love to share with others. The most loving thing we can often do for someone is remind them to love themselves.

A Soul Mate relationship will not guarantee a person a life without struggle or doubt. What it can do, however, is continue to inspire them as individuals to find their own inner strength and to encourage the strength and beauty of one another. On the etheric level, I perceive a Soul Mate relationship in this way: each individual has a spiraling double helix of light that

runs from the Cosmos down into their crown chakra and out through their feet into the earth. When the two individuals are 'sharing' light and have made a commitment on a Soul level to be with one another, the helix of light combines above their crown chakras and at their feet. Each individual remains encased in their own 'light' pillar, yet the pillar that has been created in conjunction with the partner, pulses with intensified, almost electrical, current. The individuals are energized by this pillar as if their personal power source has been doubled. Soul Mate relationships come together with a predetermined potential as agreed between two Soul groups before incarnation. Once on the earth plane in the physical body, there are different opportunities that will present themselves throughout the individuals' life. As a result of the intensity of the light that is created, Soul Mates are drawn to find one another when they have both made a free will choice in this life to offer service to humanity through their own unique gift of Love to the world. This includes Self Love.

IDENTIFYING A SOUL MATE

Very rarely will Soul Mates fail to recognize one another. If we wonder if someone is our Soul Mate, as one person seems more invested in the relationship than the other, chances are strong that this relationship is not a 'Soul Mate' one. This does not mean in feeling that someone is a Soul Mate, and their failure to say the same thing instantly, discounts the depth of the feeling, for surely we all express ourselves at varying speeds, but rather if there is a consistent draining quality to the relationship instead of an energizing quality, then the relationship is unlikely a Soul Mate one. Often times, a very strong emotional connection to a person that is not of the highest vibration, can represent a learning opportunity for removing karmic debris from a previous life path. Some souls we encounter through multiple lifetimes, the experiences from past Soul Paths, continuing to bring about opportunities for greater depths of compassion to grow. Sometimes we encounter souls for the first time that offer us a valuable opportunity to expand our self knowledge, and to practice strengthening our boundaries, or commitment to self on our soul path. In this chapter I refer to a Soul Mate in the most positive of contexts. There are soul deep meaningful encounters that people can experience through repeat incarnations together, such as the ones described in chapter two. In the context of partnership, especially romantic, if I could sum up knowing verses not knowing if the relationship is a Soul Mate relationship, the list would be as follows:

Soul Mate:

*You feel empowered together. Life feels more worthwhile and filled with possibilities.

*You find being honest comes naturally, even about insecurities, and especially about dreams.

*For whatever length of time have actually been interacting, the connection feels timeless and balanced.

Not a Soul Mate:

-You are hesitant to speak your true mind as this person has mocked you.

-You feel insulted and misunderstood often.

-You often feel as though something is missing. (This does not suggest ones partner must fill the missing piece, rather that in being with someone who wishes you to follow your Soul-path, you feel safe in expressing the desire to pursue dreams and inner truth.) *Prayer asking for assistance from Archangel Michael to overcome fear-based beliefs can aid in clearly seeing the ways in which a relationship nourishes or fails to nourish us.*

Every person, regardless of sexual orientation or ethnicity, deserves to feel it is 'safe' to stand in their own unique truth and encounter relationships that nourish and support them. Each person on the planet will be made stronger and brighter by encountering Love. On our journeys of Soul Evolution, some relationships will teach us about our strengths and some we will need to seek healing from. Yet, in the final relationships we all choose, it is my heartfelt prayer each person believes they are worthy of kindness, respect, authenticity and encouragement.

of our bodies and spirits as well as the whole planet. Diet can be a transformative process to explore, though it is most healthful when done with a conscious determination to notice fluctuations in energy levels and general health. If something we eat immediately makes us feel lethargic, explore other food alternatives. We are the master creators of our own divine health. Many people who have a passion for holistic or traditional medicine can give us encouragement and feedback, but as with the Spirit – emotional and mental – the physical body is best nurtured by a personal dedication to fostering awareness. For whatever diet we are currently feeding ourselves, here is a useful exercise to help encourage the most sustenance for our body to receive through ingestion:

*As we choose the meal, whether something someone has prepared for us or with the ingredients we are going to combine, look at each item and take a few moments to con- template the journey it has taken to reach our body. Consider the seeds that were planted by someone's hand and thank the hand that put them in the Earth. Connect with the sunlight, the wind, the bees, the water and the stars that nurtured the food's evolution.

Think of the oil used by the vehicle that brought the food to the place where we purchased it, and the people who helped to prepare it or place it on the shelves. Take a moment to thank the drivers, the grocer, the restauranteur or cook. Regardless of whether this food has arrived in a plastic or paper wrapper or has just recently been harvested from our garden, the pathway, the life of this food is all contributing to the transfer of life force that will enter our body and Being. Thank the food, the people and natural elements and ask that Love be

ingested. Ask as well that those who contributed to the evolution of the food have blessings in their day. Take the first bite as your body and Being are resonating with this thanks.

Every time I foster the time to follow this meditation of thanks and thoughtfulness, my food tastes better. The loving thoughts do add a certain 'glow' of light to the food and I find that I am more satisfied and fulfilled by the meal. When I cook for other people, the last 'spice' I add to any dish is a prayer that the food will nourish their body as well as any areas of their emotions or mind that need sustenance at this time. Many people associate food with love. Perhaps this is a primordial resonance from receiving sustenance from a mother's breast, and I honor that all food prayed over and served with love does send a particular resonance of light into the body of those who receive it.

As an example of loving affirmation, here are my favorite wishes to place over food:

★A meal for family, friends or for oneself: ★

"Dear Creator and Life force of the Planet, I ask that you send your blessings on this meal, and I thank all of the plant devas or any animals that gave of themselves to sustain those that I love and myself. Please bless this meal with the highest vibration of health and wellness so that all those who partake of it are reminded of their own unique beauty and gifts to the world. OM, Aho, Amen. Thank you."

★Preparing tea or food for those who are sick or unwell on any level (emotional pain, mental stress.) This prayer can be over glasses of water as well: ★

**"Dear God/dess, please send the healing assistance
of Archangel Raphael and Jesus to raise the vibration of this substance to the highest healing level
possible. Please send Archangel Michael to cut any
chords of fear that are attached to the person at
this time so that they may embrace their best and
brightest personal health, easily releasing any- thing
they no longer need to carry. Thank you for your
gentleness and love and thank you for bringing
about healing to this person who is so very worthy
of Divine Love and Healing. Thank you, Amen, OM
and Aho."**

NATURE AND OUR OWN REFLECTIONS

Our prayers have incredible power. Praying for all we ingest
mentally, emotionally, physically and spiritually to be a reflection
of pure Love and in accordance with our Highest Self and Soul
purpose will bring about positive change in our lives, as well as
the lives of those we interact with. I have never been sorry to utter
a prayer, but have always wanted to have said one should I have
decided for some reason that it wasn't the time. Kind thoughts,
kind words and prayers are like directing rays of sunlight onto
plants, people and nations. We are all capable of directing them
and all of us are in need of their sustenance. The people we admire
most need Light and Love; the people who challenge us the most
also need Light and Love.

During the birthing of my daughter, I experienced a lot of
fear from interactions with a particular nurse on the aspects that I
valued the most deeply. Already exhausted from 41hrs of labor and
the damage my body had undergone, my overly sensitive being
felt as though it was being punched by her words. During the
moments when I was dragging my IV back and forth down the

hallways connecting my room and the Intensive Care unit where my daughter was, I prayed incessantly.

Most of the prayers were for my daughter, a few for myself and retaining strength, but by the second day, I was also praying for the wisdom to navigate the very fear-based interactions I was having with this particular nurse. The Ascended Master Krishna brought me a message: *The most transformative prayer I could say would be for the nurse herself.* I lay in my bed, dazed and in pain, and started praying. I asked Archangel Michael to help me with the fear I was experiencing and I asked that God/dess and Jesus surround this particular nurse with Love. I asked for whatever had occurred in her life to make her fearful to be healed. They were some of the most challenging prayers I have ever formulated, yet I felt the presence of my Guardian Angels and Guides beside me, and continued with them.

The next time I wheeled my IV down the hallway, the most amazing thing happened. A friend came with me into Intensive Care and when the particular nurse I had been struggling with saw her, she blossomed. She was enthusiastic, cheerful, and informed me that she was going on days off, as well as the doctor she had been consulting with and I had been assigned to a new doctor and nurse team. I stood there and sent up a fervent prayer of gratitude. The new nurses resonated with me in kindness, the new doctor was also very kind. We were able to leave the hospital in another 24hours.

I relate this story because the birthing process was one of the most challenging physical experiences I have ever had, and my mental and emotional exhaustion was at its highest as well. Yet during this time the prayers that proved to be the most vital were not for my own well being, but for the transformation and the Divine Love of a person who was causing additional stress. In this same way, I urge people to not only pray for themselves and those that they love, but also for those who challenge them. The people who make choices that effect nations, corporations that make choices that effect the environment – pray for these leaders and CEOs to return to their hearts. Every prayer and thought pattern matters.

The power of prayer resides within every living being. I believe that animals, minerals, crystals and inanimate objects can all carry and be affected by prayer. 'Prayer' is another way of saying 'intention' or 'thought'. Think kindness or positive thoughts towards beings and they will receive those thoughts.

Just as we send our Love and Light to others, it is important to allow for the life force of the Universe and Earth to nourish and sustain us. Walk through nature. It is as simple as that. Even if our mind is racing, as we walk through the trees, the flowers or near bodies of water great or small, life force is caressing us and reaching towards our being. The world wants to resonate with radiant life and we are a part of the world. The water wants to pray for us, just as we are sending our prayers for its clarity.

The water on the planet is a powerful resonant being. As it cycles from earth to sky, it affects and connects with it all. The salt water helps to purify toxins from your bodies on all levels, and the pure water helps to energize and revitalize each cell in the body and self. More precious than the stones or minerals we base our economies and currencies on, is the water of the planet and I honor this water - the water in our cells and beings - by making choices that revitalize, cleanse and cherish its substance. Take a bath and thank the water; fill your water bottle and ask that it energize your cells. Walk by rushing water when you wish to release emotional trauma or stress, and meditate near still water to inspire and nourish your own inner calm and being. The water that falls from the sky runs beneath the earth and forms as dewdrops on the plants – it is all a precious gift. Being an advocate for clean, clear, healthy water in whatever way occurs to us, will transform us into angels for this planet and all others who reside upon and within this Earth.

WHAT CAN WE PERCEIVE AS HAPPINESS?

In accordance with the divine assistance I am receiving during the writing of this chapter, I want to explore the word 'happiness'. When I communicate with the Angels and Ascended Masters at this moment, they all 'say' in unison to focus on Happiness in its relationship and synonymous nature with Peace. If we are at peace within ourselves for choices we have made during the evolution of this particular lifetime, I believe we can honestly say we are living a 'happy' existence.

Happiness and Joy are related on the vibrational spectrum. We will all occasionally, or even frequently, be radiant with joy. We will also experience other emotions during our days and years that captivate our conscious attention, yet we are always striving for health and happiness. The Angels have encouraged me in the writing of this book to remind us that we humans can make choices each moment, day, year to live from a place based on the health and happiness of our own particular being as well as that of the planet. This does not mean each day must result in a cultural, governmental, or environmental revolution. Those are the extreme ends of the spectrum and the world will manifest them communally. It means individually we can strive to reach our own highest ideals of kindness, justice, strength of love and contributions of positive thoughts and actions that encourage the world on a grander scale. Today, for example, we may help a stranger in a small way, returning their grocery cart for them, or smiling as we pass someone on the street. That kindness, that moment of positive energy exchange, encourages them to do the same and allows for the ripple effect of that positive energy to be passed on in a universal way. We can be happy with our ability to share happiness. We can be happy with the choices we make which are premised upon the betterment of our own health, the health of our families and our communities. Striving to make conscious choices that reflect our appreciation for those around us (as well as for the Earth) – this is revolution.

It is revolutionary to commit to a path and practice of gratitude for all our blessings, to focus on nourishing the Self with Love-based thoughts of encouragement instead of ego-based thoughts of fear. We can be 'happy' that today we have done less harm and more goodness to ourselves and the world. This kind of happiness is akin to Peace and is of the same vibrational spectrum as Joy and Love. The capacity for humans to love is incredible. It is the most powerful vibration and it can, and does, change the world. There is always space for the world to have more people speaking, thinking, acting and creatively expressing their messages of Divine Love.

CHAPTER SIX

HEART MEDICINE: OUR OWN HEALING AND TRANSFORMING THE PLANET

I've often asked, 'What is the best way to heal a grieving heart?' The answer always arrives in the image of someone standing at the edge of the ocean watching waves of water undulate towards the shore. There is something so incredibly reassuring in the waves of the ocean for on some primordial level the rise and fall is not only a mirror of our inhalations and exhalations, but also of the rhythms that we experience in our lives. Sleeping and waking hours and the subconscious and conscious mind are all linked – the perfect balance for one another, changing in intensity, yet rushing towards and over us like the emotions we carry and ultimately must decide if we are ready to release when wishing to transform to another level of reality.

Likely the words, images, or sounds each individual uses to communicate a 'prayer for a bright future' will vary. Languages are a joyous dance: all vary and yet the essence of Love is universal. Each individual is capable and essential to communicating and manifesting more Love. To heal a grieving heart, we can allow the ocean of Love to soothe us. We can allow the natural world to cradle us as we witness the areas of our life or evolution that we are grieving. By allowing grief to wash through and past us, in its wake we will find greater space and capacity for Love to fill our Being and Soul. There will be times when the grief feels unbearable, and then, through the miraculous powers we possess as an individual, we metamorphasize, transform and heal. Wave after loving wave.

Healing the grief I have experienced during this life and others as well as the grief I witness in others also trying to heal is inextricably linked to the ability to experience Love on the current plane of physical manifestation as well as on a larger Soul scale. If a person is looking to transform something in their lives - to receive more love, attract abundance, share greater kindness and also to perceive it in the world around them, for example, they must first commit to acknowledging the grief they are carrying surrounding the particular issue. Is there residual grief that remains in the emotional and physical body from fear of being rejected? Is their an ego-based belief with grief surrounding not having followed ones' dreams? Archangel Raphael, an Angelic resonance of healing, as well as Aphrodite, a sea Goddess of Love, and Quan Yin a Goddess of Compassion, encourage that the grief being carried be acknowledged and released. Each offer their unique resonance on the etheric realm to soothe, encourage and cleanse the grief from our bodies on every level, creating greater space for Love to flow in.

Imagine yourself standing at the edge of a beach. The ocean is safe and brings gentle waves toward your bare feet. As the water laps at your feet, more space is created around each foot. The feet begin to allow the sand they stand upon to be sucked back with the receding waves, and invite more water to pool around them with each incoming wave. Grief can be like the sand, abrasive, uncomfortable and deeply buried. Yet the Divine Love we each have access to, both within our Souls and from the universe at large, is like the ocean. The Love sweeps the grief into soft shapes and patterns, changing the way it affects us, altering our center of balance in new and expansive ways. If we reject an opportunity for Self Love and clearing karmic debris, another wave soon follows. There will never stop being these etheric waves of Love, it is the fabric of the universe, moving towards us, washing through us and around us, each and every day.

When a relationship comes to an end, there is often the energy potential of what 'could have been' created between two people. These 'could have beens' must be grieved in order to allow for healing, release and moving forward. For example, two people may have dreamed of a home, a family and a life together. When this does not occur due to individual free will choices, the potential of the energy or of the Souls who could have been invited through the union such as birthing or adoption, leaves an energetic imprint. Through acknowledging what we had dreamed of as a possible future and releasing the grief to allow for new loving opportunities, we are set free to create an alternate future with greater joy. One of my dear friends was working through the end of an unfulfilling relationship and felt as though she had reached an energy block which she needed assistance with in her healing process. Through an Angel Reading, she was able to acknowledge that there was a potential for a child through the previous relationship, and it was this child's Soul that my friend needed to make peace with to move forward. Through acknowledging that the Soul had chosen the two of them as potential parents, and praying that the Soul find an alternate doorway into the physical plane, my friend was able to release and heal her grief. That same friend, a few years later, entered into a far more loving relationship in which the potential for multiple children exists.

Many talented physicians or holistic practitioners can offer helpful remedies for the physical body itself; there are counselors and therapists who have many gifts and tools to offer regarding the mental aspects of grief. Working with the Angels and Ascended Masters, the following chapter is intended as a tool to explore the ways in which asking for assistance on the etheric and spiritual levels can aid in the manifestation of healing at the 'heart.' It will reveal our enormous and innate capacity for receiving Divine Love and how we can feel more acutely the Love that the world and cosmos are offering each of us every minute of every day. It offers assistance in finding the strength and confidence to acknowledge grief that has been carried from previous experiences, so that the gifted individual who is each of us is able to release, transform and metamorphasize through grief into a radiant wave of Love.

FEELING CONNECTED TO HUMANITY

I had a discussion with my husband once about what would change in the world and what kind of world we would live in if one morning every person woke up and spoke exactly the truth that they were experiencing. Instead of "Hi, how are you? I am fine," interactions, what if the words were something like, "Well, today I feel sad and I'm not sure why, but instead of being at work, I wanted to just go curl up in a blanket and cry." A response of "I felt like that yesterday and many days. I wish my relationships were more fulfilling, and I want to just be myself." What a difference that day would make! A day where people acknowledged they felt challenged, vulnerable, lonely; and in return, the people they spoke to also validated their own truths about their emotional states. It is my firm belief that the day would start out on the crest of a wave of acknowledged grief but would transform in a miraculous way: that the wave would gain momentum and in these shared honesties there would be a giant overwhelming sense of Love. I believe people would feel better connected to themselves, to one another and to strangers. That sense of connection would extend to include the world at large. And on the heels of that wave would come waves of humor, hugs, encouragement and even more honesty. These waves would sparkle with the lights of deep healing which have the power to lovingly transform us and our world. It is a world I believe we are all yearning for moving towards, for the dreams that bring the greatest sense of urgency to communicate, the images I receive from the Earth and the Cosmos are all based on images that show a world wrapped in a warm, loving and transformative energy.

DREAMING THE FUTURE INTO BEING

On a recent trip to Greece, one I had long wished for and finally decided to manifest, I travelled during the off season. Many of the roads and pathways I walked across, sometimes beside, and sometimes carrying my daughter over, were silent; their cobblestones or storefronts were decorated by flowers, but very few people were present. Yet both the history and potential future of the streets were rich and filled with Souls who had traveled before and those who would visit again. The Greek people I interacted with were kind and generous with their smiles for my child. Many of the places we visited were free for entrance with a child and people were constantly offering us delicious food to eat. I felt overwhelmed with the kindness and felt very safe.

The dreams that I had of the country were vibrant. In them, women wore white which I found very interesting as in the waking present all of the women I interacted with wore black. The women in the possible future had flowers in their hair and baskets of fresh produce, flowers and food. There was a festive feeling, as if in the celebration of each day; the community and country at large was bubbling with joy. Many laughing, healthy looking children were dancing. There were open air gardens and buildings being used as progressive schools where children studied the regenerative qualities of plants and the natural work in conjunction with innovative technology. Solar panels and wind turbines were harnessing and generating electricity needed for the towns and cities. The streets did not buzz with traffic so much as hum with life and collaboration in street markets. In Athens, a giant statue of Athena had been built through a collaboration of artisans, some in their twenties and a few older artisans. The statue was of a beatific female goddess, smiling out over her city, with a bird perched on one outstretched arm. From a bird's eye view, the city was lush with greenery, some of the larger buildings also covered in green. The city had many rooftop and balcony gardens growing food; some of the abandoned buildings and ruins had been converted to community gardens as well. The possible future was sustainable and joyous.

When I talked with a tour guide who showed me and a group of other travelers through a museum and a tour of the city, she told me that many people of her age, mid to late twenties, were moving back in with their families to save money as they wanted to begin families of their own. I was very moved by her statement, as the dream I had was of incredibly strong communities raising children with multigenerational knowledge and assistance. This is something that I believe already occurs in many Greek families, and is one of the most beautiful aspects of their culture. Her comments, and the classes of children I saw while my daughter and I visited museums, were filled with bright-eyed, engaged children, who could very well become the youth, artisans and visionaries of the possible future.

Many people commented when I mentioned I was taking my three year old to Greece, that that country was unstable and did I think it was a safe idea? The Angels assured me, and so did my heart, it was an absolutely safe idea and would be a trip filled with blessings. Not only did I reconnect with energy from a previous life on Thera, but I also was blessed with images of a country that is remaking itself, a country experiencing a rise of Divine Feminine energy that will be a healing factor for its people to rise as shining examples to other cultures around the world as a future based more soulfully on regenerative earth practices, ingenuity and joy. I pray that such a future as the one I dreamed of comes to pass.

I believe the struggles that countries such as Greece and Egypt are going through are the giant waves of grief for 'humanity as a whole' – waves of clearing and releasing for the wave of Love that will follow. The Ascended Masters who have roots and seeds planted in such places, such as Aphrodite, Athena, Artemis, Hathor, Isis and Horus are all sending their particular radiance of Light towards these places and are available to any who call upon them. Whatever deity a person most resonates with, whether they follow a religion and pray most comfortably for Divine Love from Mother Mary, or whether they resonate most strongly with the Earth itself, or just in using words such as 'Divine Love" and "heart energy", all of the radiant Light is connected, collected and beamed up from Earth. Animals carry this love and these blessings, water resonates with it, and on a Soul level, we are all carriers of Divine Love and Healing. It transmits through the plants, travels across the earth on the wind and down to each of us as we sleep. When we sleep, our receptive subconscious is given greater opportunity to receive energetic transmissions. When we are awake, our conscious mind can fill our focus and daily tasks with dialogue, commentary and ego-based messages. Most people are better able to integrate energy shifts and changes as they sleep, giving themselves the opportunity for the conscious and subconscious minds to synthesize on awakening. If we plumb into this wellspring and pray, or send an intention for this Love to be accessible to those who are struggling against waves of grief, those in the midst of revolutions, or those we see on the street who appear sad, we are all connecting and utilizing the cosmic potential for metamorphosis and transformation.

Divine Love is the fabric of our physical universe. Ascended Masters, Angels, and Deities of all kinds are given names to help us tune into the particle vibration of Divine Love that we are most open to receiving at a particular time. We are able to connect with

Divine Love simply by thinking, feeling or asking for a greater awareness of it. Allowing ourselves to ask for assistance or to find magical, Love-based thoughts and feelings in what we see around us in nature and the world, will always be available to every human who has chosen to incarnate from now and into the future. The Ascended Masters and Angels associated with Love are effective for our prayers because in focusing upon them, we create an energy framework focused on Divine Love. It is through our focused intentions that we manifest the future we are dreaming into being, into the physical reality. We focus on Love and we find small ways to share this Love throughout our day. Suddenly, larger, expansive choices percolate up from these small acts, each one building upon the next until we look back and realize we have gathered the momentum of our initial dream and built an amazing mountain of Love. I dreamed of teaching my daughter yoga so that her breath would help her find balance. When she entered school I offered to teach her kindergarten class yoga. I wrote a blogpost entitled, "Peace with Children, Beauty in the World," about teaching children to breathe for Peace. Within two weeks it was shared with a university professor in Ontario and another Yoga teacher was incorporating it into her instruction of school teachers in her province about the benefits of yoga for children.

OUR HEARTS ARE THE HEARTS OF THE PLANET

We are all capable of manifesting a future for the planet based on sustainability, protection and kindness to animals, plants and our fellow human beings. We contribute to it every day by making choices on the physical plane such as what companies we support, where we buy food and what jobs we perform. On a spiritual level, each intentional thought, each dream we have for a future based upon more love helps to shield Earth from greed and fear; and those intentional thoughts and dreams work to promote Love, kindness and compassion.

Imagine Earth within a globe of Light and that the Light is radiant and pure, like fresh spring water. As we sip from this water, or as we connect with the Light, our etheric body begins to vibrate at a similar level. We then reflect this purity and our cells cleanse themselves to match the purity of the water we have sipped. On a grander scale, if we were all attuning to a more powerful vibration of Love, then countries in their entirety and the world will follow, will become part of that process of allowing the waves of grief to pass and make space for the Love that always follows.

Here are two prayers to help focus intentions and love-based manifesting - one for the Self and one for the Planet:

"Dear God/dess, Ascended Masters and Light-Based Fairy Kingdom, please help me to receive and communicate Love. I ask that you aid me on all levels of my life to perceive opportunities for positive growth. Please help me, Archangel Michael, Shiva, Durga Ma, and White Buffalo Calf Woman to feel courageous as I acknowledge the ways in which past experiences and choices have left me grieving, and help me to accept healing energy from the Earth and Cosmos of the highest vibration so that I may transform for my highest good. Thank You. Om. Amen and Aho."

"Dear God/dess and Universal Consciousness, please communicate the rays of Love and Healing to all those on the planet who are grieving or fearful at this time. Please send your highest vibrations for positive transformations to the countries, political leaders and warriors of Light to aid in the peaceful ascension of this planet for its own highest

good. I ask that my Light of Love be reflected in all those whom I interact with and that through these interactions my self, my family, my communities, my country and this world be reminded of our potential for Joy. I am a participant and advocate of Divine Compassion and I ask that these rays of Love be transmitted across this Earth to all those whose cosmic hearts are ready to transform. Thank you. Om, Amen and Aho."

The ocean of our Soul is vast and limitless. The emotions we experience are reflections of this. Emotions can sweep through us, more powerful in intensity than we imagined ourselves capable of containing. For example, when we celebrate the birth of a child, our heart can swell with more love than we knew we were capable of, reaching out to encompass and celebrate the new being. Yet at the birth of another child, the vastness of this love expands even more, our perception of all of the love we are carrying within us growing again. What we are able to perceive grows as a reflection of our willingness to similarly experience emotions such as compassion, joy and love. To acknowledge that these emotions move in wave-like patterns — to sit in stillness, or run in a passion, to express and experience them, and then allow them to peacefully transform and pass beyond our being — this is a kind of evolution. Our hearts are beautiful. They are capable of such intensities; in fact, our hearts are one of the reasons Souls come to the earth plane: to experience this intense range of emotion. Yet on a spiritual level, our base resonance is of this state: Love. Love forms the core in all beings no matter how seemingly buried. Each breath, each inhalation and exhalation is creating more space, more vital cells all wishing to communicate and celebrate this Love. As we draw our awareness to the vital cells in our physical body with intentions for Joy, Self Love, cosmic compassion and universal connections of Light, we have the power to reclaim new levels of vital health. To connect with the light grids in our physical bodies and identify areas on each level, whether physical, spiritual, emotional or mental that can be cleared through acknowledgement, forgiveness, redirection of energy, and the resonance of Love is to connect with our own capacity for Divine Healing. If we spend even a few minutes each day focusing on the ways in which we can feel our own breath fueling and healing our bodies, we are able to harness the internal divine resonance and affect incredible transformation.

CHAPTER SEVEN

MATRIX OF LIGHT, THE
INTERSECTION OF UNIVERSES

Mandalas from ancient cultures exhibit intersections of light rays that correspond to the navigation of the solar systems and universes on a grand scale and include several star systems. These light intersections connect to create an overall matrix to mirror and replicate these same intersections within our own bodies. Modern alternative health and medicinal lore can agree on a dialogue that explores the Chakras and Meridians of the body evinced in Reiki, acupuncture, yoga practice and mediation, as well as crystal and energy balancing therapies. Chakras align with master glands of the body on the physical level. Balance sought through healing on the etheric, emotional and mental bodies, can assist the physical body healing, as each of the bodies seek to resonate together. The overall link of the light body within the physical universe allows for a greater communion and understanding of the larger matrix of light as it connects this particular world, the earth plane, star systems and the multiple dimensions that the Soul travels through and communes between. The ancients built pyramids in replication of particular star and light intersections. When looking at the mandalas of ancient Tibetan, Indian or Mayan culture, one can also see these same 'maps.' In regards to the energy body, the mandalas can activate and create pathways of healing through the seven most popularly discussed chakras in a similar way that meditation, acupuncture, mantra and yoga can bring about balance. There are, however, two other important chakras which extend above the physical body that can be very powerful in effecting change, awareness, energy levels and healing. These two chakras extend above the crown chakra and the top of the head. The first is at least six inches above the crown of the head and the second eight inches above that one, yet slightly back from the center of the skull. My perception of them is as spinning golden discs. I consider the first of the two to as a filter for the frequencies of information that connect the current incarnation to the Akashic Records. The higher one functions as a bridge between the Higher Self and the Soul group of Light Beings who are working with an individual through their present incarnation to communicate in an understandable way. When the upper of the two chakras is functional, there is an active conscious awareness of the ways in which the light grid on the planet, and fellow humans, are functioning as well as an awareness of what can be done to bring about greater healing on all levels through this dimension of reality and the Cosmos at large. When these two chakras are cleared, either through sounds, light, sunlight or crystal healing, the energy level of the entire body begins to vibrate and transmit at a higher frequency. Through a devotion of time and energy to align and balance through the seven most dominant chakras, the upper two become more easily accessible to perception. The initial seven chakras are 'easier' to connect with as they align with the master glands of the body and have a very physical representation on our bodies. The upper two chakras are on the etheric plane without the physical anchor we can be accustomed to recognizing, sometimes making them 'feel' more elusive.

ASTRAL PROJECTION AND TRAVEL

As predominately clairvoyant individual, it is my intention to communicate a visualization followed by a prayer to bring awareness to the entire Light Body as well as the strong pulsing Light that continually connects our etheric selves to our much larger Soul, Higher Self and Light Beings who are present to support our current incarnation's well being and highest good.

Near the base of the Himalayas I had a very powerful dream. During an astral projection, I followed the pathway of the light chord that connects my present incarnation up through the stars to where my greater Soul, and the Light Beings with whom it works, were weaving light. Although language does not always convey the essence of an experience, I do endeavor to communicate in the most positive way possible this experience, and I pray the words will evoke a feeling or a resonant experience for the reader on a heart level should my language and images not be equal to the task.

The 'weaving' was a joint intentional creation of energy and opportunity being spun together by a balanced group of high vibrational beings. These beings had agreed to work together to send Light and energy down toward the Earth and into the conscious or subconscious minds to the Souls presently incarnated. I perceived the figures as seated in a lotus position, because, I believe, it would be an easily interpreted image for a human to return with. They were surrounded by stars and looked down into a large pool of light. The stars stretched across the sky and all sides of the figures including beneath their suspended forms and the light pool. Surrounding them, translucent with the stars shining through, were similar shapes of the Himalayas. I as a human currently in the Himalayas, was made to feel safe although I was witnessing something far vaster than my human consciousness experienced on the physical plane. I have often visited different dimensions where I 'received' Light-based messages and the vibration present

71

is similar to the discernible AUM sound held in much of the Earth, particularly sacred mountains. This same vibrational frequency can saturate the Spirit body while in the etheric realm, and when it is present I am always sure that my journey will be a safe one. As in previous experiences, I felt safe and capable of returning to my body. Through viewing the matrix of Light intersections that combine and connect to weave together the present and future realties, I was able to better 'see' Life as a transformative Soul experience, far vaster than a single incarnation and human eyes would allow. To witness and feel connected to this co-creation of reality, allows me to appreciate the interconnectedness of all Souls' potential for manifesting a peaceful, abundant life on this planet and in this star system.

WHAT WE BRING BACK

The message that I believe is most important to convey about our human existence is that when we come together in a meditative or prayerful state, we are connecting with our Higher Selves, with the larger Soul that is our root Being and all the Light that exists on the Angelic, God/dess Ascended Master plane. Additionally, it connects us to further dimensions which hold all Light. In this connection we are all capable of manifesting incredible change. An elevation of awareness through mass prayer or meditation, a relaxing of the mental experience to a heart-centered communion with the Divine, creates a direct link through all of the chakras down into the Earth and up through the crown to the upper chakras that receive and transmit radiant energy.

EMPOWERING THE SELF TO ATTUNE AND RECEIVE

To begin a visualization that activates and clears through the upper chakras, it is encouraged that the body has digested healthful and high vibrational food such as vegetables and fruit as well as plenty of pure water. I strongly urge as well that all visualization occur in nature or a space that feels very 'safe'. If that space is in the home, choose a room cleansed with fresh flowers or the branches from a spruce, cedar or pine tree to elevate the energy of the room.

Finding a comfortable position, whether laying flat or seated, we ask particular guardian angels – the Archangel Michael for protection, and the Archangel Raphael for healing – for their presence. If at any point during the visualization there is a feeling of 'fear,' ask that God/dess and the protective light of Archangel Michael clear the space surrounding the body and Self with blue fiery light. If there is a difficulty visualizing colors, consider dressing in a strong blue that day. The body is most grounded when it has a clear flowing energy between itself and the Earth as well as with the other chakras. I feel an alignment of all of the chakras begin when I have an Epsom salt bath, swim in the ocean or find a stream of sunlight to sit in while breathing with intention.

Breathing with intention can be achieved by placing the hands with interlaced fingers over the belly button. By connecting with our power center, we are actively seeking to find a balanced flow between all of the chakras. This enables us to begin an overall alignment from a place of personal power. Emotional trauma and other fear-based thoughts can block each of the chakras, so it is important to honor all of them, beginning at the root chakra to create a solid foundation for being grounded and ending at the two chakras above the head for the energy within the body to be released and received in a clear flowing manner that promotes optimum health and vibrational harmony. The energy from the universe is received through the upper chakras and into the head. It circulates through the body and down into the earth, connecting with the energy of the planet, as well as receiving energy from the planet, that is then synthesized in the bodies and released on a cosmic level in communion with the universal life force of the cosmos. When I assist someone with their healing journey, I prefer to touch their feet at the beginning of a session as well as at the end. This enables them to reconnect with their bodies and to assimilate the transfer and transformations of energy that they have allowed for during a meditative or relaxed state. To ground in a warm climate, allow for your bare feet to touch and press into the Earth; or if seated cross-legged, allowing for the expansion of the root chakra down through the sit bones into the soil, sand, or rock is effective. If it is winter, or one is inside, consider wearing natural fibers on the feet for socks, such as organic cotton or ethically gathered wool.

WORKING WITH THE CHAKRAS
FROM THE ROOT UPWARDS

Imagine a beautiful globe of light at the base of the spine connected by two bands of the same light which extend through each foot and deep down into the Earth. Take a moment to thank our Earth for cradling each of our footsteps, and honor the ways in which we move and travel across the face of it. There are seed sounds associated with each chakra as well as balancing crystals and musical chords. Finding a crystal healing book or searching out a singing bowl recording that resonates with you can be beneficial on your individual journey. I feel grounded when working with the turquoise stone, or when using my singing bowl. A simple seed sound from the Hatha yogic tradition accompanies each chakra.

THE ROOT CHAKRA CAN BE BALANCED WITH A REPETITION OF
OM VAM
(SOUNDS LIKE AUM VUM)

Next allow the light bands to spiral up to the sacral chakra where they encounter another spinning wheel of light. This light is beautiful and Archangel Raphael is standing with us, offering any healing that we wish to allow at the space where our creativity and sexuality exist. All light globes will rotate at a similar speed in the chakras, and if we sense that one of the globes is shifting to balance itself through changing its size to harmonize with the others, allow this as it is a healthy occurrence. As the Angels protect and nourish us, we release any karmic, emotional, mental or spiritual debris that is affecting the health of our chakras.

THE SECOND CHAKRA CAN BE BALANCED WITH OM LAM (SOUNDS LIKE AUM LUM)

As the light expands further, it fills and cleanses through our stomach. This is the chakra connected to our personal sense of power and our assertive, powerful nature. This chakra can manifest cleansing as bowel movements in the days following the visualization and it is important to nourish and aid this cleanse through high vibrational food, tea or juices.

THE THIRD CHAKRA BALANCES WITH OM RAM (SOUNDS LIKE AUM RUM)

Traveling and expanding upwards, this brilliant, radiant, healing light fills our heart. We may notice that our lungs expand, our breath deepens and our shoulders naturally roll back as we feel the grace of Divine Love traveling to and from our body. This light will activate naturally the upper heart chakra that is between the throat and heart center; if we find ourselves swallowing or coughing, it is just a natural cleansing process. We remember to take our time, each chakra will require different levels of awareness and light healing as we all assimilate the human experience in different ways.

THE FOURTH CHAKRA SOUND IS OM YAM (SOUNDS LIKE AUM YUM)

Taking sips of water if we are feeling parched and being gentle with the Self in all ways, next the throat chakra will be cleansing and filling with light. This globe of light may make our ears pop as the upper and lower chakras begin to connect and the energy flows more naturally between them. Our throat chakra enables us to speak our truth, to sing our song, to whisper, shout, or howl our joy as it clears. Mantra and song are particularly healthy ways of stimulating throat chakra health.

THE FIFTH CHAKRA IS OM HAM
(SOUNDS LIKE AUM HUM)

As the light expands upwards through the third eye, it is normal for images from life, or new perceptions from situations that have occurred on other realms, to cleanse themselves. The third eye is our ability to perceive Truth in different layers of reality. Archangels Metatron and Uriel are always available to aid in the facilitation of clear intuition and cleansing at the third eye.

THE SOUND OF THE SIXTH CHAKRA IS OM OM
(SOUNDS LIKE AUM AUM)

Next the crown chakra may begin to feel as though it is tingling. This light, as it has expanded up through the body from the Earth is helping to open the perceptions of the Universe and the ability for the bodies on each level to assimilate Light and Divine encouragement. The light at the crown chakra has often been depicted like a thousand petal lotus opening, and so too, do the levels of our awareness and our limitless capacity for growth opens and expands at this place. The debris at the crown chakra that can accumulate from receiving and sensitivity to mass consciousness as a whole can feel heavy, cause headaches and make us feel exhausted.

THE SOUND FOR THE SEVENTH CHAKRA IS OM FOLLOWED BY SILENCE, WHICH MAKES SPACE FOR THE HIGHER VIBRATIONS OF THE COSMOS.

To cleanse this chakra, allow the light globe of the chakra to spin and expand above the head, connecting to the upper chakra that is about six inches above it. These two chakras, when synchronized with the third will often manifest as brilliant white light. When they are cleared and spinning in unison, energy from the Universe is then able to assimilate down through all of the other chakras and complete the spiral of Light that is rooting into the earth. Visually we may perceive our Light body as these chakras and pinpoints of light, all connected by a pure and resonant double spiral of light. The Light spiral forms a band extending up to the Soul and Higher Self and a shield of Light like a tube of brilliant colors surrounding all of the bodies with the double helix shape running up through the center. This visualization of our Light has incredible healing potential.

There are particular crystal bowl or prayer bowl sounds that can work specifically with these chakras, but the most accessible balancing is available through the first rays of soft sunlight at sunrise. The gentle light is excellent for clearing them, and simply sitting in the sunlight inside or outside and thinking of them with an intention of healing is encouraged.

PRAYER-FULL RESONANCE

When in a state of meditation and balance through all of the light chakras, while connected to the Earth and the two higher levels of the Soul, we are all capable of perceiving our own communion and relevance with the Divine. We are able to see the world in new ways and to interact with fellow humans and Souls at the highest, heart-centered place of connection and healing. After such visualization, it is normal to need a nap or, conversely, to feel highly energized. Some people may process change best while sleeping as it allows the conscious mind to give way and the subconscious mind to re-assimilate itself. Others may want to run through a forest, swim across a lake or dance beneath the stars. The intensity of transformation through clearing chakras and connection to the Universe at large will reverberate throughout our human experience and offer the opportunity for powerful change. This visualization can also occur after a full body balancing yoga practice or a massage experience delivered by a safe and committed practitioner. It can also happen after extended time out in nature. By nourishing the body with pure water, loving relationships and Self-care on every level, the energy we experience for change and transformation will continue to support our journey.

Our bodies and beings strive for health, healing and high vibrational existence. All health is connected to the Light that is a stream of energy through Being, the Earth and the Cosmos.

CHAPTER EIGHT

DUALITY AND INNER KNOWING

The Angels speak to us of Peace, Love and inner Knowing. They remind us that it is within our Divine connection and magnificent Souls to have the power for transmutation to transform our lives, our intentions and energies into new or alternate realities.

I like to think of the ultimate in alchemical magic to be a person's choice to change their life and infuse the areas that have caused them pain, or the lessons they are ready to release and to change the energy within themselves into 'gold'. By changing our own internal vibration, the external world begins to vibrate and manifest at an equal rate. Then new opportunities, change and growth occurs. When looking at the internal energies of people around me who make a conscious choice to change their lives by beginning with their internal selves, my etheric eyes perceive this intention like liquid gold, or flowing honey, infusing their being and beginning to radiate outwards. When a person is vibrating in such a way, they also act like a beacon for those around them who are curious or yearning for self-transformation as well. When engaged in a transformational period, it is particularly important to maintain 'healthy boundaries' for during transformation we can feel extremely open and vulnerable.

The following is a blog post from my website: compassion-angelcardreading.com.

BOUNDARIES AND PERSONAL POWER

Boundaries are healthy intentions to create and keep a sacred space around the 'self' and energy field. Like a plant in the warmth of the sun, the more we invest and strengthen our 'boundaries', the stronger and healthier they become. Having a 'boundary' that allows us to acknowledge what is healthy and supportive of our life purpose, daily interactions and evolving relationships is challenging, yet attainable.

To create and explore our own unique sacred space, I offer this visualization:

Retreat to a place that feels 'safe' – this could be outside, or inside, but is best practiced alone, or at least alone within a twelve-foot radius. Interlace the fingers and place them over the solar plexus and begin to relax into deeper breathing.

When our lungs and body feel as though they are saturated in oxygen, choose a vibrant color that resonates at this time with us. This color should be bright and make us feel safe, healthy and vital when we see or wear it.

Imagine that we have picked up a giant paintbrush and drawn a circle around our self. This circle touches the ground, leaving space between us and the surrounding world. The line the paint- brush leaves is thick and strong. If we need to draw the circle more than once to feel that it is solid, do so. Once drawn, take a moment to set an intention/ or prayer. Something like this:

"I ask that God(dess), my Higher Self, my Guides, my Guardian Angels and the Ascended Masters and Earth Helpers help to clear my energy field from any negativity and fear that I no longer wish to carry. In this circle of Light, I reconnect with my Being, Life purpose, and immense Divine Love. Thank you for the assistance on every level. Amen, Om and Aho."

By enclosing ourselves in a circle of light, we have not stopped loving, or being connected with those in our life we love. Instead we have created a stronger inner ability to experience love and center our self.

Perhaps as our day progresses we will feel this circle shrink, it might begin to fit our body like a shield of armor, or it may be challenged as we interact with those who are used to trespassing on our boundaries. If we tune into our inner knowing throughout the day, even for a few moments, and do a visual scan of what is happening with our circle of light after such interactions, and if necessary, draw the circle with our giant mental paintbrush once more. Drawing an energy boundary takes practice. At first it may need to be consciously thought of at the forefront of the mental focus every few minutes, or hour, yet with practice it becomes instantaneous and can be present at all times of the day.

Ideally this 'boundary drawing' will become routine. The colors may change with the seasons, our spiritual journey, or our mood and life experiences. When the colors are vibrant, they are feeding and protecting us simultaneously.

Some of the Angelic, Ascended Master hues are:

Archangel Michael, Shiva or Christ Consciousness works primarily with dynamic blue for safety, and protection.

Archangel Jophiel and Quan Yin have hues of pink that lead to seeing the beauty within the self and the world.

Archangel Raphael and Buddha are predominantly green or gold hues, bringing healing on all levels to those that work with them.

Archangel Ariel, Lao Tzu and Saraswati often bring gold and white light for transformation and release of burdens.

We all possess the ability to be energetically sensitive and aware. We all deserve to be nourished internally before sharing our gifts with the world around us. Healthy boundaries lead to healthy relationships in all aspects of one's life. May we have excellent Health!

TRANSFORMATIONAL PLANET

Mass consciousness is evolving. Each person, whether on a subconscious or conscious level, is becoming increasingly more sensitive to the 'sixth sense' – the spiritual or energetic reality of the Universe. As they do so, healing and grief can occur, and the process, although represented by the Mother Earth herself along with the shifting and re-growth She has been stimulating, can feel overwhelming. By focusing on the internal journey of each of our Spirits and Souls through trusting the small and large messages from the Angels and Guides, the Fairy Kingdom and the Animals are attempting to communicate everyday, we have the potential to be radiant gold Light-filled beings who ignite a network of Light that reaches across the planet and far out into the Cosmos. When we are doing so, it is important to ask for assistance from those whom we trust, not only on the etheric plane, but also from one another in terms of asking for more gentleness, more patience, more encouragement and positive communication. We are all capable of being joyous. Perhaps not every single day, as life will continually offer us all opportunities to grow, but at our inner place of internal resonance and flame of the Soul, we exist in a state of Joy.

It is my heartfelt wish that during these chapters there has been something that spoke and reminded each reader that they possess the Knowing, Light, and power of Divine transformation, and that though their bodies my pose challenges, above all, their Spirit is vast and perfect.

With that in mind, I offer a blessing from the **Divine Feminine** with the assistance of the **Blessed Mother Mary** as well as **Pele and Isis:**

> "You who have swum from my bosom to this world, know that I cradle you still, though not only with soft and encouraging arms, but also with the strength and courage you have gained through your many lifetimes and realities. I am the arms that are close at hand, to catch you should you fall, yet cheering for you and helping to spread your etheric wings, for I have faith in your success. People of the planet, return to the Love and Light that resides within your breath, for your breath is the wind that brings change. Your heartbeat is the heartbeat of the Earth. Speak out, for your voices united can move mountains, and the blessed Mother, the fiery Goddess and the resurrecting Winged One all are here in this moment as qualities that reside within you. AUM, Amen and Aho."

With assistance from **Jesus, Poseidon, and Buddha**, a blessing of the **Divine Masculine:**

> "You who are strong in your gentleness and generous in your learning, you the travelers who have offered to share your bread and your hearts, it is time to step forward to encourage your Brothers and Sisters of the Planet to be kind instead of crushing and to celebrate the power of non-violence. Be as the mighty mountain, firm in your protection of the beauty within your Soul and the mirroring Souls in those who surround you. Reach

out your ingenuity of creation to build that which
sustains the Earth and Her people. From the stars,
the sky, the wind and the rain, this is a time of
great cleansing; and all who resonate with Light
are needed, appreciated and supported. We are with
you, within you and communicating daily. Speak
your truth and listen to the truth of others, for
you are a bridge with one another that can span
the lengths and depths of this Planet. Om, Amen,
and Aho."

We are each a beautiful compilation, a rainbow of Light, that
is balanced in divine masculine and feminine attributes. To dance
with inner joy, honoring the ways in which our own divine masculine and feminine wish to be expressed. People, partners, romantic relationships all will mirror back this inner joy, but none can
truly heal another's inner energy. It is a conscious choice to be a
strong woman who has a balanced strong masculine within her
being and a strong man who allows for a balanced and expressive
internal divine feminine. We are multifaceted, multidimensional
beings, and in this celebration of our own, and one another's gifts,
we are a chorus of Divine Joy.

So today, and everyday, may your resonant Joy spill over into
your waking and conscious Life; and may the courage, conviction
and truth of your own Soul path, powers of Healing and transformation be sustained and nourished and magnified.

The world is waiting for us all. Shine.

AFTERWARDS

It has been an extreme honor to facilitate and express these messages during all of the chapters. Thank you for your collaboration for a healing Self, Planet and Cosmos!

With devotion to God/dess, in recognition of those who have come before and those who will follow, the Angels, Ascended Masters, Fairies, Animals and Plants, I thank you all for sharing your sustaining Light. To the "inner children" of Light workers who are adults, and for the children who are blessing the planet with their presence, thank you for your Light! Although this world may seem daunting, I place my faith in your ability to transform it.

From my heart,
Kamia Shepherd

BONUS MATERIAL

ASTRAL PROJECTION TO SHAMBALA

As a child, I would have described myself as a 'vivid dreamer'. As I grew older, I began to discern the difference between what I considered a 'dream' and what was more like an astral projection. I believe astral projection can be described as when the Spirit travels from the body to another time or place to collect and retain information, knowledge and details once returned to the waking world.

Many of my astral projection experiences bring me into the presence of Ascended Masters and the gifts they wish to share with all of us humans. Their teachings are similar to the ones they offered when they walked the Earth before ascending, but I find there is a vivid distilling of their messages that imparts greater clarity and essence.

The last three days I have been spending time while 'sleeping' learning with Lao Tzu. When he told me his name, I asked him to spell it so I could look it up. Sure enough, Google reveals some sketches of him that look very much like the benevolent smiling older man who stood before me on a rocky pass in the Himalayas robed in soft golds and oranges.

To meet him, I walked through a cave and out onto a steep trail across a valley where I was looking at what some would call 'Shambala', or – as I like to think of it – a future dimension the world is working towards as one possible reality that coexists with our own, even now. In it there are small cities with dome shaped buildings, pure water, and acres upon acres of green space: gardens, orchards and small fields. The view was beautiful, but what Lao Tzu wanted to share with me was a waterfall directly beside the exit of the cave passageway. This waterfall was not like a waterfall in our dimension/reality. It was made from silver and gold light and inside of it he indicated I could clear the lower energies 'sticking' to my aura.

I have stood under this waterfall off and on for the last three days. I've slept more than 55 of the last 72 hours. Today I am feeling enlivened. I feel 'lighter,' more centered in my Self and my inner Knowing. The essence of the waterfall can be accessed through prayer and visualization. With the guidance and permission of Lao Tzu, I share the following:

For anyone who is ready to release fearful or lower energies that make them feel cold or tired, unfocused or ungrounded from themselves, it is an honor to share this prayer with you:

"Dear God/dess Force, and Universal Energy of Creation, please help me to clear all lower energies that are effecting my well being at this time. Please surround me in a spiral of gold and white Light that reactivates the cellular reconstruction of each of my bodies for its highest vibrational potential and good. Please bring me the assistance and guidance of the Ascended Masters who resonate with my Soul Path, to usher in time, space and healing that I am ready for in a gentle manner. Please help me to retain any images, songs, feelings or thoughts that are messages from these benevolent Guides. With deep Love and Respect, Om, Amen and Aho. Thank You."

I recommend a position for meditation where you have created a sacred space with time to processes any changes or adjustments that need to occur. If you are new to energy work, then the prayer can be said before bed and if you have been troubled with insomnia lately, try a few drops of lavender essential oil near your beside to encourage peaceful and soothing sleep.

The Ascended Masters are very close to the Earth and to our consciousness at this time. They have walked the Earth, they remember the struggles, the suffering, and the inconsistencies of being human. They bring gifts of non-judgment and compassion. They are free in their energy bodies to be with everyone at once and are not limited by time or space. If you feel drawn to one in particular, they are most likely with you through this entire Soul Path as they recognize an affinity with your Life Purpose. For example, I have always loved Quan Yin, and felt drawn to images of her. In my minds eye she is robed in flowing silk -like light, in pinks of every hue, with a lotus flower below her, and arms reaching outwards to enfold those before her with compassion and grace. I also feel that bringing and living with Compassion is a large part of my Soul Path and purpose just as it is one of the attributes Quan Yin brings to the Earth.

People often believe they are not special enough, not worthy enough of the notice of Angelic, or Ascended Masters. This is untrue. Each person comes through to the Earth with a wide array of Guides, Angels, Ascended Masters, Spirit Helpers, Ancestors, Fairies and Elementals who resonate and work with them. You, the person reading this, have a team. Feeling connected to ones etheric support team can shift ones reality in incredible ways. Instead of feeling lonely, one begins to perceive that there is always a loving group surrounding one, ready with support and encouragement. The support team I work with such as the fairies and angels who give practical advice, or the ascended masters and ancestors I receive doses of humor as well as strength from, all surround my earth experience when I am willing to connect with them. I find a greater balance within myself, when receiving the messages, and remember more frequently to expand my view of life, which allows me to celebrate the beauty, and acknowledge the sorrow. I have said to myself, and will undoubtedly say again, "I can't". The etheric support team 'shouts' back, "YES, you can!" People who doubt they have etheric support teams can connect with them sometimes most easily, in nature. Visit a place one finds exquisitely beautiful, as one appreciates this beauty, the feelings of self worth, often begin to expand. The self worth rising, allows the connection to the beauty of nature, as well as the 'clearer' etheric space that has been created for divine love from ones higher self, and the etheric support team, to flow more freely into one's Self.

The world continues to shift. We witness others around us acting with hate and pain. We see sorrows and we feel empathy and despair. Yet the world is also shifting with Light. There are acts of love and kindness that occur. There are people speaking their truth and working towards a more peaceful and loving planet.

Each of us has the power of free will. To chose each day in each situation to ask, 'Will I bring more kindness? Will I act with compassion, with peace?' Our choices matter: individually, universally and cosmically. Claim space and time to sit and connect with the higher source of your Self to allow your Soul to be cleansed of the lower energies in your aura, and to rebirth in your day, Peace. You are worthy. This world is worth it, now and for our combined future.

Shanti Om,
With light, Kamia

HEALING PAST LIFE RELATIONSHIPS
FOR PRESENT LIFE WELLNESS

Some of the hardest relationships to let go of, either in friendship or as romantic partnerships, are those in which we are connecting with a Soul from a past life in which one of us died a significant amount of time ahead of the other. One of the Souls then spent several years mourning the loss of the companionship, and as Light often calls to Light, another lifetime has come into being in which we are attracted to one another. In some cases this can be a healthy reunion, built around mutual respect, affection and supreme love. In other cases however, some of the emotional debris from the previous life can muddy and complicate the present incarnations' relationship in an unhealthy, yet seemingly inextricable way.

An example of this might be of two friends of a similar age, yet one of which requires a lot of 'mothering' from the other. Although neither need to be a mother in this life, one constantly is the recipient of the late night requests for problem solving and seems to continuously require a fountain of nurturing. With meditation and prayer, one of the friends has a vivid memory of being a parent in a previous lifetime. In this scenario, as in all others of such a reunion, it takes two people determined to be actively aware of themselves and their energy bodies to help heal the wounds from the past and move forward into a brighter future together. If only one Soul wants to grow into a new bond in this present life the relationship cannot continue.

Identifying these kinds of relationships can be accomplished by praying before sleep for a message, image or dream to recognize the previous lifetime. If you are an individual who does not often remember dreams, it can be accomplished by seeking out an energy worker, CERTIFIED ANGEL CARD READER (R) or psychic you feel safe and comfortable with. Ask them to 'read' the energy surrounding the relationship. A few strong indicators that a connection has unresolved karmic debris from other lifetimes influencing the present day interactions are:

1. You feel exhausted after casual interactions with a person.

2. A relationship 'feels' far more intensely real to you than the other person seems to be feeling in return. Your desire for a deeper Soul level connection is rejected repeatedly by this person and they seem not to understand you.

3. You have never met a person before, yet the first time you lay eyes on them you experience a very intense emotional response (love, fear, anger, yearning, surprise, a full spectrum of all and more).

A positive prayer to release past life trauma and heal karmic debris is:

"I call on my Higher Self, Angelic Helpers, God/dess and Spiritual Guides and Guardians to please help to surround me in a spiral of Light. I ask that all past trauma in relationship with [*insert name*] be healed for the mutual and individual benefit of us both. I pray that on a Soul level we are able to forgive and be forgiven by one another so that our Divine Life Purpose in this present life can be

celebrated and met. Thank you, Angels for helping to clear my energy in this way; I receive your blessings of health on all levels with open arms and heart. Om, Amen and Aho"

During this prayer, envision a spiral of light surrounding your body from the tips of your toes to the sky. It can be a combination of vibrant colors or gleaming, white light. As the spiral circulates, allow the 'debris to be sucked into it and carried up into the sky where it can be transformed by the Angelic realm. Notice any areas in the body that experience momentary lightness or a relief of pain and be gentle with them. Take an Epsom salt bath and indulge in self nurturing. Just as taking off a bandage can reveal tender skin, so too can healing karmic wounds leave the Self feeling newly vulnerable.

If this prayer creates a positive change in ones own self-esteem, it is important to be aware that we all heal in different ways and at different stages. If the person you wish to heal with begins to drift away from you, sometimes the last stage of healing is that you let one another go. If the Souls have truly healed the past life trauma, then they each have the opportunity to begin a new learning experience together based on mutual love and respect, or to attract new learning and evolutionary experiences with other Light Beings. Letting go can be sad, it can release grief from both or many lifetimes together, yet I promise you, that the greatest of loves never die. They are always and already brilliant colors on the energetic plane that still connect the Souls who feel them. True love is limitless and supports the individual Soul Path of each of us. If the love was from the purest part of the Soul, then it continues to connect us past and through new lifetimes and across the boundaries of the physical world.

With light and respect for your journey,
Kamia.

CHOICE CENTERING AND
RECONCILIATION OF SELF

There are many instances in life where we as humans can experience a sense of powerlessness. Yet even in these instances, we are powerful. We are powerful beings in that we always have the choice of how we as individuals and as expansive souls choose to act or re-act. Instead of fixating our energy on what it is that makes us feel powerless, such as a job opportunity or relationship that is not playing out in accordance with the script we have in our minds, we can choose to release our desire to control and allow for an expansion of our energies, our life opportunities and ultimately our happiness. We do this by choosing to reconnect with our 'center' and perceive life and the world on a grander scale.

When I limit my vision, I experience frustration with finances, daily tasks or relationships, but when I 'look' from my center, I perceive the blessings in my life, the opportunities for growth, the choices I have made and can continue to make to nurture authentic relationships. From my human eyes I see a town or an empty street, but from my center I perceive my place on the planet, the energy that connects me to the continent to which I am standing and spreads out on the lay lines of light that connect this continent with each other and the water that flows between it all. Finding a balance between the duality of existing in this present reality and honoring the greater reality we are all manifesting is a personal and global phenomenon we all must explore.

In the spirit of this exploration I offer this exercise and visualization with the assistance of Archangel Haniel who is the Angel carrying messages and gifts that connect humanity with the 'grace of God/dess' and their own Divine Light.

"Dear God/dess, Universal Consciousness and my Higher Self, please help me to connect to the Light that resides within my Being and this Earth. Please send me assistance through Archangel Haniel and any other Ascended Master I am most aligned with at this time through clear signs, images and feelings to help me to perceive the grander scale of my life purpose, the gifts I have to offer to the planet, and the daily joy and difference I can make through my choices. Please help me to spread my wings of light, to expand my consciousness like a swan flying upwards into the sky and truly 'see' that this planet holds incredible beauty to which I am an integral contributor. Thank you, Amen and Om."

Each human has Divine Light within them and our daily choices reflect, encourage or shelter this Light. When we return to our 'center' we feel encouraged to make healthful choices throughout our day and lives that nourish our own brilliance, gifts and Divine Joy. From a centered place, researching options for a different job, letting go of an energetically draining relationship, or exploring a move to a new location all seem possible and manageable. The center of our Being knows that hard work and determination, Self kindness and Self respect are all natural elements of our personality and Higher Soul.

May your find your center today. And should you need a helping hand, know that the Guardian Angels who surround you and the Earth beneath your feet, are all reaching towards you to hug, cradle and support you in being 'centered' and aligned for your own, as well as the planet's, highest vibration of Joy.

With light and respect for your journey,
Kamia

INNOCENCE AND RELATIONSHIP

Many times in life, the ego asserts itself with punishing words and self-blame that is unfair and unfounded. It is important to develop an internal dialogue that brings the ego back into balance and fosters an inner warrior-ship that defends the innocence we all carry. Innocence, as I recently communicated to a client, is not the same as naivete.

Innocence is the ability to see the absolute Light and Love within the Self, another Self or a situation and our faith that anything can be transformed. It is with Innocence that we often leap forward to tell someone or share with someone in relationship (can be friendship) all of the potential and gifts we believe they carry. It is with Innocence that we find the courage to have faith in ourselves, to attempt a new class, new career, move or trip. When we watch a child discover the magic of the world, to talk to the animals and unseen fairies as friends, to speak of the dreams they have, we are reminded of the innate Innocence that they carry and we ourselves carry.

Foster this beautiful attribute within yourself. Make a list of the dreams you have that are based on this purity of heart, and repeat, as many times as it takes, "I deserve to trust and believe in my worthiness to foster this beautiful vision within my Self".

I often see those around me, stepping forward to act in honor of their own belief in others' Light, particularly in relationship. Sometimes this Light is not as consciously honored in the partner or individual they want to beam themselves at. This does not mean that they were wrong in believing the other was deserving of this Light, recognition, or faith. Sometimes it means that the other is not as aware of their own Light and are not capable at this time of reflecting it back to you. You have given them a gift in sharing yourself and your faith in this way. Foster this gift by allowing them to continue on their path in hopes that they may find the means of honoring themselves in a similar way one day. Foster your inner innocence by moving forward in search of relationships that are as equally nourishing of the Self as you are willing to be of another.

We are all born Innocent, sometimes circumstance and experience dampens this brilliant light within, but no matter what, it is still within you. The Angels reach around you in a gentle hug to safeguard and reignite the spark. See the world this way for a day, see the light within all others, and remember, you are shining, every moment of every day. The Angels acknowledge this; it is time to acknowledge it yourself.

With Love,
Kamia

ABOUT THE AUTHOR

Kamia Shepherd was raised in the Canadian Rockies in this life by two Old Soul parents and three interesting older siblings she also recognized from past lives. She was fortunate to encounter many spiritual seekers at an early age and benefited from their individual gifts of energy work, astrology, medicine wheel gatherings, sweat ceremonies, drumming circles, clairvoyance and healing touch. Seeking to expand her awareness of herself, she dedicated a decade to traveling the world. Communing with Nature, Ascended Masters, Angels and Fairies in such countries as Nepal, China, India, Cambodia, Thailand, Vietnam, Laos, Costa Rica, Guatemala, Nicaragua, Honduras, Peru, Bolivia, Chile, USA, Cuba, Greece, Italy and Mexico, was a gift that in part lead to this book. It took Kamia until her late twenties to feel confident enough to share her clairvoyant gifts with the world at large. A seeker of spiritual truths, mother, wife, ANGEL THERAPY PRACTITIONER(R), Hatha Yoga Teacher, and nature enthusiast, she looks forward to continuing to share wisdom with the world through both writing and speaking on the etheric realms and the Divine Love she believes is accessible to all living beings.

To connect with Kamia visit:

compassionangelcardreading.com
for personal readings and new monthly blogposts

Kamia Shepherd Compassion on Facebook

@kamiashepherd on Instagram

Compassion and Soul Evolution with Kamia on Pinterest

compassionkamia808 on Youtube

ARTIST INFORMATION

To request limited edition prints of the artwork featured in Soul Evolution, from artist Jane Shepherd, please email **greywolf2@ live.ca** or contact Kamia.

CPSIA information can be obtained
at www.ICGtesting.com
Printed in the USA
LVIC06n2338150216
475227LV00002B/2